The AWARE Saga
Civil Society and Public Morality in Singapore

The AWARE Saga
Civil Society and Public Morality in Singapore

Edited by

Terence Chong

NUS PRESS
SINGAPORE

Published by:

NUS Press
National University of Singapore
AS3-01-02, 3 Arts Link
Singapore 117569

Fax: (65) 6774-0652
E-mail: nusbooks@nus.edu.sg
Website: http://www.nus.edu.sg/nuspress

ISBN 978-9971-69-551-4 (Paper)

National Library Board, Singapore Cataloguing-in-Publication Data

The AWARE saga: civil society and public morality in Singapore / edited by
    Terence Chong. – Singapore: NUS Press, c2011.
    p. cm.
    Includes index.
    ISBN: 978-9971-69-551-4 (pbk.)

    1. Association of Women for Action and Research. 2. Civil society –
Singapore. 3. Religion and civil society – Singapore. 4. Social ethics –
Singapore. I. Chong, Terence.

JC337
300.95957 — dc22   OCN707605528

Cover: Supporters at AWARE EGM on 2 May 2009 (Photograph courtesy of
    AWARE).

Typeset by: Scientifik Graphics
Printed by: Mainland Press Pte Ltd

CONTENTS

Introduction

Terence Chong

On 28 March 2009 a group of Christian women took over the country's most well-known women's rights group, sparking a chain of events that not only enthralled the nation but also forced many to re-examine the way they viewed civil society politics in Singapore. There were already signs that it was not going to be another routine evening when an unexpectedly large number of people attended the annual general meeting of the Association of Women for Action and Research (AWARE), many of whom were new faces having only joined the NGO in recent months. Of the 12 available seats on the executive committee (Exco), the new members captured nine, leaving the so-called "old guard" shocked and confused.[1] Adding to the confusion was Claire Nazar's sudden and unexplained resignation on 8 April as AWARE's new president just 11 days later after her unopposed election.[2] The public only knew of these events when the local media broke the story on 10 April (*The Straits Times* 10 April 2009).

With Nazar's resignation, the old guard, led by immediate past president Constance Singam, rallied some 160 members on 14 April to call for an extraordinary meeting, possibly to table a motion of no confidence in the new Exco given its reluctance to answer questions about who they were, how they got together to takeover the NGO and what direction they intended to take it. A day later, on 15 April, the new Exco met to pick a new president — Josie Lau. Things took an even more puzzling turn when Lau's employer, DBS Bank, immediately issued a statement noting that it did not support her taking up the presidency and had told her so.

The next day, two-time AWARE president Braema Mathi was informed by the new Exco via email that she was no longer in charge of producing a report on discrimination against women in Singapore. That same day, DBS Bank issued *yet* another public statement revealing that Lau had breached its staff code of conduct twice by not informing her

1

superiors that she had intended to stand for AWARE's elections and for ignoring the bank's advice against taking up the presidency. It warned that it did not condone such conduct from its staff and promised an internal review (*The Straits Times* 17 April 2009). By this time, the local media had uncovered an intriguing link between some of the new members of the Exco — six out of nine of them attended the same church, the Anglican Church of Our Saviour (COOS) located at Margaret Drive (*The Straits Times* 18 April 2009). They were Josie Lau, Charlotte Wong (the new vice-president), Jenica Chua (new honorary secretary), Sally Ang (assistant honorary treasurer), Maureen Ong (honorary treasurer), and Irene Yee (committee member). In addition, the local media also found them to hold trenchant anti-homosexual and anti-abortion views. One of the new Exco members, Jenica Chua, had written letters to the press to argue against normalising homosexuality and to admonish a Nominated Member of Parliament (NMP) for championing gay rights in Parliament.[3]

Facing the growing chorus of questions from the public and old guard members, the new guard convened a press conference on 23 April. By this time it was clear to everyone that the label "old guard", ironic in the context of this saga, stood for progressive values and liberal attitudes while "new guard" denoted moral conservatism and hetero-sexual orthodoxies. The stage was set for high drama. With a theatrical flourish, senior lawyer and former dean of the former Singapore University law faculty, Dr Thio Su Mien, came forward to introduce herself as "Feminist Mentor" to the new Exco. Thio, also a member of COOS, told the reporters present that she had encouraged the women to take over AWARE because she felt it had shifted its focus from gender equality to the promotion of homosexuality and lesbianism. She went on to attack AWARE's sex education syllabus, under the Ministry of Education's (MOE) Comprehensive Sex Education (CSE) programme, for encouraging local students to see homosexuality in 'neutral' terms instead of 'negatively', and warned that "this is something which should concern parents in Singapore. Are we going to have an entire genera-tion of lesbians?" (*The Straits Times* 24 April 2009a).[4] The drama at the press conference heightened when the new Exco announced that, since the saga went public, Jenica Chua and Alan Chin, anti-homosexual campaigner and Josie Lau's husband, had been on the receiving end of death threats. And to top off the spectacle, Chew I-Jin, one of only two members of the new Exco from the old guard, burst into the room protesting how the Exco had not informed her of the press conference.

She was told by Lois Ng, one of the new Exco, "As you're an old guard member, and the old guard have had a field day giving the media stories upon stories which are totally and utterly inaccurate, this is our chance to talk to the media. So I would appreciate that you leave this room" (*The Straits Times* 24 April 2009b). Meanwhile, the old guard had discovered that the new Exco had changed the locks and security system at the AWARE Centre in Dover Crescent.

Singaporeans began to take sides as the saga gained momentum with extensive media coverage. An online "Save AWARE Campaign" petition with close to 400 signatures was formed to urge supporters to attend the extraordinary general meeting (EGM) scheduled for 2 May to consider a vote of no confidence in the new Exco. A variety of blogs and online forums accused the new Exco of orchestrating a "hostile" takeover to further their own agenda and berated its link to "fundamentalist churches" (*The Straits Times* 24 April 2009c). On the other side of the fence, numerous letters in support of the new Exco appeared in the press. A typical letter observed that "The CVs of the new Exco members show that they are responsible women with high educational achievements, and good families and marriages, who are committed to social work. The new committee seems very qualified for AWARE's declared objectives, namely, the guardian of women's rights in Singapore and a group with programmes and avenues to foster better treatment of women" (*The Straits Times* 24 April 2009d). Others were more direct: "The truth is out. Schools should not invite the group to talk about sexuality if they are pro-gay. The whole saga has shown that gays are organised and infiltrating groups that may have influence on society. I call on the authorities to close AWARE as it will no longer be credible after this" (*The Straits Times* 25 April 2009a).

In response to Thio's allegations, the MOE initially defended AWARE's sex education programme. The Director of Education Programmes wrote to the press noting that the "schools that engaged AWARE found that the content and messages of the sessions conducted were appropriate for their students and adhered to guidelines to respect the values of different religious groups", and that the schools did not receive any negative feedback from students or parents (*The Straits Times* 29 April 2009). However, on 6 May, the MOE suspended AWARE's programme. The Ministry announced that some of the suggested responses in the instructor's manual for AWARE's programme were "too explicit and inappropriate, and convey messages which could promote homosexuality or suggest approval of pre-marital sex" (*The Straits Times* 6 May 2009).

Members of the public contributed to the debate on several levels. Some questioned the role of the media in playing up the saga, some supported the new Exco's agenda but condemned the way it came to power, some celebrated the public interest the saga garnered as a demonstration of civic passion, while others deplored the old guard's neutral stance on homosexuality as symptomatic of society's eroding moral values. Nevertheless, as the twin issues of Christianity and homosexuality echoed louder and with greater frequency, public memories of the 2007 parliamentary debate over the repeal of 377A were stirred.[5] Sensing the deepening societal cleavages over the saga, the Singapore government stated its stance. Deputy Prime Minister Teo Chee Hean called for the two camps "to show respect and tolerance for each other's views", while Lim Hwee Hua, Minister in the Prime Minister's Office, urged all involved not to "allow these disagreements to become a vehicle for views on contentious, divisive issues to be pushed aggressively. This would polarise our society and have a very adverse effect on our social fabric" (*The Straits Times* 25 April 2009b). Minister for Community Development, Youth and Sport, Vivian Balakrishnan, told the press that it was "potentially dangerous for religion to descend into the fray of petty politics", but stressed "that the Government would not be getting involved at this point in time" (*The Straits Times* 27 April 2009). Meanwhile, even the venue of the EGM did not escape controversy. The new Exco had initially chosen a hall in Toa Payoh but later changed its mind and designated the Singapore Expo in Changi as venue. This sparked rumours that the change was made to coincide with a mega Christian conference that was taking place at the Expo on the weekend of the EGM; a conference that COOS was part of. The police finally intervened and the venue was changed again, this time to Suntec City International Convention and Exhibition Centre, for law and order concerns. By this time, AWARE's membership had soared from 300 before the saga to 3,000 just before the EGM, with both camps urging its supporters to join up to make their voices heard.

The emotional stakes were unexpectedly raised a day before the EGM. *The Straits Times* reported that COOS Senior Pastor Derek Hong had, in a sermon to his congregation, "urged the women in his flock to 'be engaged' and support Ms Lau and 'her sisters' at AWARE" (*The Straits Times* 1 May 2009a). In the same sermon Pastor Hong was quoted as saying: "It's not a crusade against the people but there's a line that God has drawn for us, and we don't want our nation crossing that line" (ibid.). Understandably, his remarks drew indignation from the public, prompting Archbishop Dr John Chew, head of the National Council of Churches of Singapore (NCCS), to issue a public statement warning churches to stay out of the saga. "We do not condone churches getting involved in this matter; neither do we condone pulpits being used for this purpose" (*The Straits Times* 1 May 2009b). Dr Chew's public statement and Pastor Hong's subsequent expression of "regret" over his remarks served to ease tensions a little, and may have even affected the Christian turnout at the EGM.

There was an air of expectation among the nearly 3,000 members who descended on Suntec City Hall 402. The EGM began inauspiciously when committee member Lois Ng demanded that Siew Kum Hong, NMP and the old guard's "legal advisor", who was seated among the women, join the men who were on the other side of the auditorium. Josie Lau's attempt at an introductory speech as president was cut short when members from the floor rose to tell her that her three minute speaking time was up. As the heckling from the audience grew in volume, the new Exco demanded that security remove those responsible, and when this did not happen, Sally Ang, assistant honorary secretary shouted at AWARE old guard member Margaret Thomas to "shut up and sit down". The booing did not stop when Thio Su Mien stood up to speak. Citing her mention on "page 73" in a 2007 AWARE publication and her experience as the first woman law dean, she demanded that the noisy crowd "Show some respect to your elders" (*The Straits Times* 3 May 2009). It quickly became clear that the majority of the audience were in favour of the old guard and were much more vocal than those who came in support of the new Exco; the former dressed in white shirts and the latter in red shirts. It was rumoured that larger numbers of new Exco supporters were meant to attend the meeting but did not because of Dr Chew's last minute intervention. One of the many questions levelled at the new Exco was the amount of money it had spent thus far. There was an audible gasp when honorary treasurer Maureen Ong gave the estimated figure to be S$90,000. The list of expenses included rental of the convention hall, security systems at the AWARE Centre, security guards for the EGM and lawyer fees to Rajah & Tann. This figure far exceeded the S$20,000 limit that the Exco was authorised to spend in a month. After much haranguing, the motion of no confidence was finally put to the vote. And at the end of an EGM that lasted nearly seven hours, the motion of no confidence was passed 1,414 votes to 761. Josie Lau and the new Exco, though not legally obliged to step down, did so on the advice of its lawyers, bringing the saga to an end.[6]

* * *

The debates that the AWARE saga sparked saw public discussions ranging from the place of religion in civil society, gay rights, the processes of citizenry mobilisation, the activist role of the media and the undeniable liberal voice in contemporary Singapore. Never before had a single event ushered so many issues into the public sphere for such a rare display of political pluralism so often cloaked by the aegis of a one-party state. This political pluralism, many times manifesting boisterously, was invariably viewed by some as anathema to the grand narrative of Singapore politics where the initial top-down control of society in the early years had evolved into a more "consensual" and "non-confrontational" style of state-society relations. The different actors in the saga found support from their respective constituencies, many of whom were vociferous and even strident in their championing of the issues at stake, revealing a kaleidoscope of political and cultural identities at odds with each other. To a large extent, the saga succeeded in rupturing the many interpellations of Singaporeans by the People's Action Party (PAP) state, from that of a coherent society with "Shared values" to one which was steeped in "Asian values". The socio-cultural fault lines that were exposed as the saga unfolded not only suggested that the gulf between social reality and state-sponsored constructs of nationhood was wide, but also that unless greater acknowledgement in terms of public discussion was paid to the increasingly fragmenting nature of local identity politics, much of which was a reflection of global struggles, Singaporeans would not acquire the maturity to resist framing the occasional political-ideological conflict as nothing less than a national crisis.

One could even argue that the AWARE saga and the way it exploded into national consciousness was the cumulative result after years of downplaying individualism and identity politics and, instead, playing up social harmony thus plastering over societal cracks with constant references to our multicultural façade. Recent incidents suggest that this is more of a trend than an aberration: In early 2010, Senior Pastor Rony Tan of Lighthouse Evangelism, a mega church, was caught denigrating the Buddhist and Taoist faith in a sermon on Youtube (*The Straits*

Times 9 Feb. 2010). A few months later, another mega church pastor, Mark Ng of New Creation, was seen mocking the Taoist faith where he compared the praying to Taoist deities to "seeking protection from secret society gangsters" (*The Straits Times* 15 June 2010). Indeed, one deeper concern was how the AWARE saga took many by surprise and how the depth of feelings and the passions it aroused caught political observers and the government off guard. The fact that the saga's two vital ingredients — aggressive Christian activism and gay rights — were not new and had been fermenting in our midst for at least a decade or two only serves to underline the dangers of overstating the city-state's multicultural complexion at the expense of addressing the undeniable intolerance and uncompromising stance of certain communities even if their members may be over-represented in positions of political power in Singapore.

Nonetheless, it is in the nature of the one-party state to exude stability. It is in its interest to interpret the AWARE saga as an aberration in a society where government and societal attention and energies must be studiously channelled towards ensuring a trajectory of economic growth and development. And yet, the AWARE saga *is* the very child of economic growth and the expanding middle class it has engendered. Over 40 years of mass education, economic progress, and world travel have nurtured an increased attentiveness to one's personal rights, and heightened sensitivity to encroachments on individual freedoms and progressive values. It would be wishful thinking to expect a sophisticated and cosmopolitan-minded polity to display the same manner of acquiescence and political faith their parents did, especially when such issues strike so deeply into matters of identity and ideology.

If anything, this saga has provided greater analytical texture to the political character of the Singapore middle class. Often seen as dependent on the state and its distribution of wealth, the local middle class has generally been characterised as politically compliant and an anomaly to the theory that an expanding middle class will gravitate towards a more liberal democracy. Instead, it has been forcefully argued that neither the western model of progress towards liberal democracy nor the Asian model of traditional communitarianism describes the Singapore middle class, but more influential to its political character is the "kiasuism" or an anxiety that stems from the lack of self-confidence and "managerial rationalism" which values "good governance" (Jones and Brown 1994). However, much has happened since the early 1990s when such arguments were prevalent. Global and regional events like the 1997 Asian financial crisis, September 11, SARS, the global financial crisis have set the background for uncertainty and change, while the recent political developments in Malaysia, Thailand and Indonesia demonstrate that the *status quo* may be successfully challenged. Domestically speaking, there has been an undeniable increase in acts of civil disobedience, online critical commentary and films.

All this is not to suggest that the Singapore middle class is now ready to take the lead in local politics but that it is widening the public space for critique and criticism. And it is in this widened space that the middle class expresses itself politically through the prism of identity politics like religious values, notions of morality, sexual politics and ideological worldviews. It may be argued that the high expectations and scrutiny that come with Singapore party politics, and the potential consequences if one is not on the right side has made identity politics a far more attractive strategy for influencing public policies. For instance, some of the greatest resistance to recent policy decisions such as the building of the two casinos in the Integrated Resorts, Section 377A, and censorship liberalisation in the arts, have come not from opposition political parties but from religious conservatives, suggesting that the real question is not whether religion can be kept separate from politics but if the political process has, as it is narrowly defined and proscribed by the PAP state, alienated sections of the Singapore middle class.

And there have been ample incubation sites for identity politics. Religion and race, on one hand, are sacred sites in multicultural Singapore, out-of-bounds from external critique, thus allowing identities and values to form without challenge, while the greater leeway granted to more liberal spheres like local theatre and the arts to articulate sexual politics and alternative lifestyles has allowed them to serve as a site where intellectual energies may converge. Such sites have allowed identity politics to develop and mature, and have become crucial spaces for mobilisation and activism. And the AWARE saga should be understood in this context. Not as a one-off aberration or a middle class ready to push the political envelope but a specific condition of society where identity politics offers an alternative to party politics in the effort to influence public policy. In many ways, the AWARE saga is important not for the event itself but for the many social trends and forces that came together for a perfect storm. These social trends and forces, brewing over decades of economic growth and socio-political change, deserve analytical attention because they offer a broader, more historical and contextual explanation for the AWARE saga. It is with this perspective that this book was commissioned.

The opening two chapters consciously adopt historical perspectives in order to paint for the reader a broad picture of the contemporary socio-political landscape that nurtured the forces and trends which came together in the AWARE saga. In broad strokes, they attempt to explain how the forces of liberalism, conservatism, morality and competition have formed over the decades so as to set the scene for discussion. Chua Beng Huat's chapter examines how the logic of meritocracy has, over the decades, nurtured economic individualism and liberal individual rights in freedom of belief and self-expression. Chua argues that the latter has often been under-analysed because scholars and commentators have often been distracted by the authoritarian state, and it has taken the AWARE saga to "make Singapore's liberal base visible", so to speak. Chua concludes that although the AWARE saga was a triumph of liberalism over conservatism, it would be wrong to presume that Singapore was now a liberal society. Instead, it is still a predominantly conservative society under a dominant ruling party that will have to contend with the seemingly unstoppable liberalisation of culture and identity politics in Singapore. Terence Chong argues that the PAP has been proficient in constructing itself as a "moral state" for political and economic imperatives, and this has been useful in accommodating the interests of moral and religious conservatives throughout the industrialising years. However, in the last decade or so, there has been a shift in the PAP state's moral discourse such that, instead of leading the charge on moral matters, it now takes a back seat and looks to society for cues on moral trends. This perceived "abdication" of the moralistic state has left a vacuum which both conservatives and liberals alike have rushed in to fill. The Christian takeover of AWARE and their watchfulness over MOE's CSE programme are thus signs of how moral conservatives feel the need to compensate for the absence of the moralistic state.

Azhar Ghani and Gillian Koh examine the state's role in the saga. They observe that the state's initial "*laissez-faire* approach" during the takeover was in line with its stated aim of encouraging more active civic participation. It did not matter to the government whether AWARE was administered by the old guard or new guard since the legal and policy status of homosexuality was clear. The moment for state intervention was when Senior Pastor Derek Hong made his "God has drawn a line for us" sermon; and while the shadow of religion had always loomed large throughout the saga, Hong's sermon was nothing less than a clarion call to mobilise fellow Christians. Azhar and Koh's interviews show that Internal Security Department (ISD) officers paid a visit to Archbishop Dr John Chew, head of the NCCS, immediately after Hong's sermon was publicised, thus prompting him to issue the statement distancing the Christian Church from Hong's remarks. They conclude that state intervention was carefully calibrated such that civic participation would not be discouraged while religious mobilisation and politicking were nipped in the bud. Eugene K.B. Tan surveys the Christian community's response to the saga. Tan traces the role of religion in the conflict, and contrasts the response of the National Council of Churches of Singapore with that of the Catholic Archdiocese in Singapore to demonstrate the nuanced politics with regards to civil society and morality. He concludes that religion has a place in civil society and that while Singaporeans are entitled to their beliefs and values, the actions flowing from such beliefs and values must not offend the imperative of maintaining and enhancing the foundational principles of our society. Dominic Chua, James Koh and Jack Yong look at the politics surrounding the Comprehensive Sex Education (CSE) programme. They assert that the new guard shares many similarities with the Christian Right movement in the U.S., and explore the discursive strategies employed by the new guard to challenge and demonise AWARE's CSE programme. They argue that such strategies organised ambivalence, confusion and anxieties about sexuality into tidy sound bites designed for mass mobilisation, thus leaving more complex understandings of sexuality out of public discussion. Loh Chee Kong reviews the role of the media throughout the saga. Loh notes that while the "investigative journalism" demonstrated by the media drew some criticism from the government, the new guard did themselves no favours by appearing to be reticent, in contrast to the old guard whose members were obviously more comfortable with the media. This initial reticence may have cast the image of the new guard as evasive in stone, thus setting up clear heroes and villains for public consumption. Loh concludes that the Singapore media is caught between a rock and a hard place in a fast-changing society still bound by stiff media regulations.

Alex Tham explores the AWARE takeover from an organisational perspective. He observes that "network forms" of organisations like AWARE are inclusive and derive their strength from diversity. Internal conflict and contestation can be accommodated because action is oriented by the values driving the work than on results *per se*. Tham argues that such a pluralist organisation was at stake during the takeover because the new guard closely resembled a "hierarchical organisation" where action tends to be instrumental. In such organisations conflict is deemed to be unproductive and a deviation from the norm, and to prevent such deviations, they place a premium on homogeneity which, Tham concludes, would dismantle what AWARE stands for. Theresa Devasahayam continues with the theme of inclusiveness and diversity in her examination of feminism and the way it was contested by both sides. She argues that feminism was a site of ideological conflict between the old guard, which propounded economic and sexual diversity, and the new guard which tried to redefine "feminism" in terms of hetero-normativity. Lai Ah Eng offers an ethnographic account of the 2 May EGM. As an insider-outsider observer, Lai leverages on her twin roles as old guard member of AWARE and anthropologist to describe the run-up to the EGM and the event itself as the performance of civil society. Finally, Vivienne Wee explores notions of secularity and pluralism. Wee notes that secularity and pluralism can no longer be taken for granted as implicit assumptions, but should be made explicit, thus enabling greater discourse and understanding over the organisation's public role.

While this book is not a comprehensive survey of the saga, nor does it strive to be, it seeks to offer the reader two things. First, a political and historical context in which to situate this complex conflict and, second, an intelligent discussion on the various intriguing threads that ran through the saga. It is a book for laypersons and scholars alike who wonder what the conflict between liberalism and conservatism, rising religiosity and the desire to create a more moral society means for a multicultural Singapore.

Notes

1. New members of the AWARE executive committee were Charlotte Wong Hock Soon (vice president), Jenica Chua Chor Ping (honorary secretary), Sally Ang Koon Hian (assistant honorary secretary), Maureen Ong Lee Keang (honorary treasurer), Catherine Tan Ling Ghim (committee member), Lois Ng (committee member), Irene Yee Khor Quin (committee member) and Peggy Leong Pek Kay (committee member). Old members who remained in the executive committee were Caris Lim (committee member) and Chew I-Jin (assistant honorary treasurer).

2. She later told the media she quit over the new Exco's "stormtrooper tactics" (*The Straits Times* 19 April 2009).
3. Chua's letters were published in *The Straits Times*, 25 May 2007 and 7 Oct. 2007.
4. It may seem that Thio and the new guard have achieved their objective. In April 2010, MOE announced that six organisations would be awarded the contract to conduct sex education classes in local schools. Of the six, four have clear links to Christian organisations (*The Straits Times* 29 April 2010).
5. Section 377A of the Penal Code criminalises sex between men.
6. Josie Lau has since left DBS bank to join the hospitality group, Overseas Union Enterprise (OUE). OUE is led by Thio Su Mien's husband, Thio Gim Hock (*Channel News Asia* 26 Sept. 2009).

References

Channel News Asia, 26 Sept. 2009, "Former AWARE President Josie Lau leaves DBS", <http://www.channelnewsasia.com/stories/singaporelocalnews/view/1007388/1/.html> [accessed 26 Sept. 2009].

Jones, David Martin and Brown, David, 1994, "Singapore and the myth of the liberalizing middle class", *The Pacific Review* 7 (1): 79-87.

The Straits Times, 25 May 2007, "Some erroneous claims in writer's views on gay debate", by Jenica Chua.

————, 17 Oct. 2007, "NMP overstepped role in championing gay cause", by Jenica Chua.

————, 10 April 2009, "Unknowns knock out veterans at AWARE polls", by Wong Kim Hoh.

————, 17 April 2009, "DBS tells why it rebuked Josie Lau", by Wong Kim Hoh.

————, 18 April 2009, "Some attend the same church", by Tan Dawn Wei.

————, 19 April 2009, "Claire Nazar: Why I quit as AWARE President", by Serene Goh.

————, 24 April 2009a, "Dr Thio upset about sexuality programme", by Zakir Hussain.

————, 24 April 2009b, "Long-time member and new Exco lock horns", by Radha Basu.

————, 24 April 2009c, "Petition against new AWARE", by Derrick Ho.

————, 24 April 2009d, "Well suited for job", Forum Page, by Gwenda Loong.

————, 25 April 2009a, "Schools should not invite group to give sex talks", Forum Page (Online), by Tan Siew Cheng.

————, 25 April 2009b, "AWARE rift: Govt leaders call for tolerance", by Robin Chan and Jamie Ee.

_____, 27 April 2009, "Keep religion above 'petty politics', says Vivian", by Li Xueying.

_____, 29 April 2009, "MOE: No complaints from parents, Dr Thio", Forum Page, by Sum Chee Wah Director, Education Programmes, Ministry of Education.

_____, 1 May 2009a, "Church against homosexuality as 'normal alternative lifestyle'", by Nur Dianah Suhaimi.

_____, 1 May 2009b, "Churches should stay out of AWARE tussle", by Zakir Hussain and Wong Kim Hoh.

_____, 3 May 2009, "'Feminist mentor' responds to jibes", by Sandra Davie.

_____, 6 May 2009, "AWARE sex guide suspended", by Diana Othman.

_____, 9 Feb. 2010, "Pastor called up by ISD", by Yen Feng.

_____, 29 April 2010, "Ministry picks groups to teach sexuality education", by Teo Shang Long and Liew Hanqing.

_____, 15 June 2010, "Church pastor apologies", Yen Feng.

CHAPTER 1

Making Singapore's Liberal Base Visible

Chua Beng Huat

Introduction

Singapore is a postcolonial society with particularistic characteristics. Historical evidence showed that the island was a trade centre in the fourteenth century when it was Temasek. However, by the time of Stamford Raffles' arrival it was no more than a tiny settlement, which facilitated Raffles' bringing the island under the absolute control of the East India Company and its later transfer to the British colonial office. With the founding of the trading post, waves of immigrants came from China, South Asia and the islands of Malay Archipelago. Singapore was a settler country, with a multiracial immigrant population. The colonisation of Singapore island did not result in the destruction of a local economy, indigenous culture or pre-modern state/government system. Without an indigenous state prior to British colonisation, there were no traditional leaders that could readily claim the right to govern; there was no past political system that could be dusted off and reinstated as the government system. No bloody war of independence was fought; consequently there were no military leaders who could claim political leadership and establish a military regime, on account of having shed blood for the new nation. The island-state, declared independent on 9 August 1965, had to be constituted entirely on the template of a modern state.

In the midst of the Cold War, two models of modern state formation were available for emulation: the liberal democratic state of the so-called Free World or the Communist State. Having been through a decade of "Emergency War" with the Malayan Communist Party, from the end of Japanese Occupation in 1946 to Malaya independence in 1957, Malaysia would not accept a communist Singapore. Neither would Indonesia, which was in the midst of the bloodiest massacre of communists and their alleged or real fellow travellers, nor the Philippines, where the Communist Party remains an organised insurgent force. Besides, the People's Action Party (PAP) itself had been through an internal struggle between the allegedly pro-communist left faction and the English-university-educated social democrats within the party that led to the splitting of the left-wing to form *Barisan Socialis*. Not surprisingly, the Constitution of the Republic of Singapore is one that contains all the individual rights and freedoms of a liberal democracy, with a significant difference: Singapore is to be a "multiracial" nation and there is to be racial equality.

Framing Governance: Repression, Race and Religion

The PAP had already begun to consolidate its power from the point it formed the first elected parliament in 1959. Political suppression included prolong jailing of alleged communists under the Internal Security Act which allows for detention without trial, and deregistering radical labour unions, replacing them with government-backed industrial unions under the National Trades Union Congress (NTUC). With the PAP–NTUC partnership, industrial "peace" was imposed — workers' rights trimmed and employers' rights expanded — making Singapore attractive to foreign capital to drive the nascent industrialisation. In 1968, the left-wing politicians who remained outside prisons committed collective political suicide by refusing to partake in the general elections. This last rash act gave the PAP its first absolute parliamentary majority and control of the state, with periodic adjustments to electoral procedures needed to maintain this absolute hold on power. Repressive authoritarianism was at its most vehement during the 1960s and 1970s. This was "condoned" internationally by the Cold War atmosphere. Against the 1965 massacre of alleged communists in Indonesia, the ten-year insurgency in Malaya (1946–56), and the long revolutionary war in Vietnam, political detentions in Singapore were rather minor offences and as such drew little, if any, condemnation from the liberal nations of the West. Subsequently, in the past two decades, political suppression of dissent became more sporadic and targeted against specific individuals; nevertheless, threat of suppression continues to cast long shadows on the population. Collective memories of the past remain undiminished; the increased use of defamation suits as a means of controlling dissent and criticisms provides evidence of continuing repression.

Race is another area where intense government intervention was evident from the start. The reality of the three racial groups is translated into a basis of governance in many areas of social life. In contrast to the logic of liberal individual rights, constitutionally equality of race operates on the logic of group rights. For example, "mother-tongue" languages are given equal emphasis in school. In the logic of equality of groups, individual preferences are of little concern; until recently, competency in mother-tongue language was required for entrance to local tertiary education. Politically, the PAP government is obsessively preoccupied with the threat to racial peace and harmony, incessantly recalling the 1964 race riots to remind all that racial violence is always around the corner if vigilance to keep it at bay slackened. Race is the fault-line that calls for active governance and policing, including criminalisation of racial chauvinism.

Religion overlaps with race in a complex manner: Hinduism is exclusively Indian, but Indians can be Muslims, Buddhists or Christians. Chinese can convert into any religion; they may, and many do, pray in Hindu temples but Hinduism disallows conversion. Malay is made coterminous with Islam, by Constitution. Likening religious conflicts with racial violence, the boundaries between different religions are sites of government policing; the Maintenance of Religious Harmony Act prohibits offensive proselytising and insensitive attempts at conversion to avoid conflict; Islam does not allow conversion while Christians are duty bound to convert others. Legal constraints on religion as public institutions are couched in terms of modern state, that is the separation of religion and politics. However, the PAP government does not strictly abide by this injunction as Islam exclusively is politically represented directly in parliament by the Minister of Muslim Affairs. Nevertheless, the PAP government accepts the liberal individual right and freedom of belief.

Meanwhile, as it is the medium of education Singaporeans has become increasingly English-speaking and literate. This is justified because it is the language by which success and failure are sorted out and individualised. It serves the logic of meritocracy. Of course, instrumental justification of English as merely the language of public administration and commerce is naïve, if not disingenuous. Inevitably, it becomes the language by which individuals formulate and articulate their social and cultural values. Two developments are significant. First, national interests come to be articulated increasingly through English, as the other official Asian languages become increasingly identified with the interests of their respective races. Second, especially for tertiary-educated Singaporeans, abstract values become increasingly expressed in English. English affords ready access to the language of individualism, reinforced by the ideology of meritocracy which justifies subjective rights, desires and demands, in contrast to the conservative values taught in Asian languages and promoted as cultural ballast and heritage.

In sum, the political sphere is framed by two sets of factors. On the one hand, it is framed by a collective memory of repression and on-going occasional instances of suppression of dissent and public debates in issues of race and religion. This constitutes the authoritarianism of the PAP state. On the other hand, the logic of meritocracy promotes liberal economic individualism, and of liberal individual rights in freedom of belief and of self-expression, albeit heavily circumscribed by laws that govern race and religion. This liberalism is diffused and veiled by the conventionally obsessive criticism of authoritarianism; a liberalism that the AWARE event made visible.

Liberalising Culture

At the contact zones of these two logics, in areas not covered by formal politics, public race and/or public religion, is the space for small "p" political activities and political subject formation, in what is conventionally known as civil society. This is the area of "cultural politics" writ small, where choice is given greatest freedom as subjective preferences, as self-expression of lifestyles and identities. In the politics of culture, choice is supreme, liberalism rules. Led by and responding to a general global condition, Singapore has undoubtedly been liberalising the cultural sphere.

While student rebellions in Asia were mainly bloody confrontations with authoritarian regimes, such as the Thammasat University massacre of 6 October 1973 and the Burmese student rebellion of 8 August 1988, the long 1960s social revolution, on university campuses and the streets in the West, spawned a string of new social "liberation" movements, including the Women's Liberation movement, which later morphed into the Feminist movement, and engendered the Gay Rights movement. These new social movements reconfigured conventional conceptions of social order and re-imagined the world as desired rather than accepting the world as given. The feminist movement detached the concept of gender from its conventional equation with biological sex. Gender was exposed as a historically determined and socially con-structed phenomenon for which biological sex is merely an excuse, an ideological alibi, to keep women in a socially unequal and disadvan-taged position relative to men. The most immediate contestation for any women's organisation is to liberate women from subordination. This was a primary motivating force in the founding of AWARE in the early 1980s.

Meanwhile, deeper social changes had been taking place in Singa-pore although these were often missed or dismissed by political critics who had their eyes fixated on the unchanging PAP-dominated single-party parliamentary political structure. With 40 years of continuous economic expansion built in large measure on an increasingly educated work force, society has become far too complex to be contained by authoritarianism — social class differences have become more visible with the emergence of a growing middle class; consumerism has affected everyone, generating a plethora of lifestyle choices, the body has become a locus of status display through food consumption and adornment; exposed to different cultural beliefs and practices, not least liberal Western ideas, personal beliefs have varied, fragmenting any remnants of shared values; overall, self-identity has become an aesthetic work in progress. This liberalisation of culture and liberal self-formation is a dynamic process that does not look back but only looks forward; personal preferences and desires kept expanding and changing, trans-gressing limits after limits.

Forced by circumstance, the PAP government has responded pro-actively to the social change by way of promoting "culture", not sur-prisingly, cast in terms of improving the nation's attractiveness to globally mobile talents who might be attracted to work here. During his watch, PM Goh Chok Tong aimed for "a culturally vibrant society, defined as one whose people are well-informed, creative, sensitive and gracious". A whole slew of arts institutions was established: the Ministry of Information, Communication and the Arts (MICA), the National Arts Council (NAC), several museums under the National Heritage Board, new campuses for the Nanyang Academy of Fine Arts and LaSalle Art Institute, the Esplanade–Theatres on the Bay, a new National Library and a new secondary School for the Arts. In addition to the annual

Singapore Arts Festival, the Singapore Biennale is now part of the arts calendar. The visibility of the "high" culture promotion garnered positive international publicity. *TIME* magazine, Asian edition (19 July 1999), declared on its cover, "Singapore Swings"; inside, it writes "the city-state is getting competitive, creative and even funky". Music to the ears of the PAP leadership better known for their straitlaced, no-nonsense and morally righteous governance!

Government support is partly a mode of incorporating the arts into its economic and political calculus. But arts and artists are not easily digestible. Art in all its modalities privileges itself as a practice in examining the complexities of social life, raising issues, criticising conventional practices, testing and transgressing conventional boundaries, pushing the limits of mainstream and government-promoted ideological concepts. The battleground is censorship. If an artistic criticism passes without comment from relevant public agencies, it is a moment of liberalising culture and liberation for its practitioner. If a challenged authority chooses to censor or enforce modification of the artistic practice, it shows its repressive hands and by extension, the repressiveness of the state, calling attention and raising public interests and debates. Hence, in spite of the government's moral conservatism, public agencies are increasingly reluctant to exercise censorship. Furthermore, agencies with the mandate to promote culture have, with an eye on their own interests, contributed to liberalising the cultural sphere.

A relevant example is the history of the women-centred play *Talaq* (Islamic word for divorce), a monologue composed from "true life experiences of voiceless minority Indian (Tamil) Muslim women [that] explores the issue of adultery, marital violence and rape, oppression and culture of silence forced upon these women by their kith and kin, dominant males and community".[1] Although the play had been staged twice before and the NAC had provided funding for the publication of the play in English and Tamil, a public entertainment license for staging the play separately in English and Malay was denied in October 2002, on grounds of "religious sensitivities". Arguably, the NAC was forced to recommend banning because of the theatre group's uncompromising resistance to a preview of the play by, among others, all male members from Indian Muslim organisations. The theatre group had anticipated the preview would result either in serious censoring or an outright ban. The ban unavoidably detracted from the credibility of NAC and the government as supporters of the arts. The confrontation of freedom of the arts and protest from "offended" religious individuals and groups in this incident may be said to have anticipated the AWARE incident.

In general, sexuality is a conventionally tabooed topic on which artists and theatre groups are bound to focus their critiques. Through the 1990s, sexual-theme theatre performances were common — nudity, gays and lesbian pleasures and anguish, AIDS. Notably AIDS infected Paddy Chew's monologue, *Completely With/Out Character*, staged by The Necessary Stage in 1999. Liberalisation of sexual content was not restricted to "high-brow" theatre but was taking place in popular cultural spheres too. The film rating system minimises censorship on sex and violence. Bar-top and/or pole dancing were permitted not only in pubs in entertainment strips but also local kopitiams in housing estates and, in 2009, as part of the National Day Parade performances, was euphemistically renamed "pole acrobatics". Geylang became a "hard-to-believe" site for tourist-voyeurs who have only known the moralising Singapore, and an open sex market for others. The Singapore Tourist Board was not against internationally organised gay parties, since they brought in pink dollars, until the organisers became too blatant and they became embarrassing to the government and were banned in 2004. Then, the government revealed that there are gays among civil servants. The gay community and its sympathisers capitalised on this momentum with the petition to repeal the Victorian, colonial anti-homosexual law. The law, nonetheless, stays as an empty symbolic gesture to appease the conservatives and/or religious even though the gay community secured the government's promise that it will not police or prosecute homosexuality among consenting adults. The liberalisation of polymorphous sexuality, as in all liberalisations, is a one-way street towards greater freedoms.

AWARE

As mentioned earlier, AWARE was a new social movement for advocacy for gender equality that has a legitimate claim in political liberalism. In the area of equal rights advocacy it had been relatively successful: the inequality of fringe benefits in the civil service is now history. On issues of men's violence — both perceptual psychological and actual physical — against women, AWARE has been successful in placing these on the agenda for public debate; for example, campaigning against sexist advertisements, establishing a rape crisis hotline and counseling for victims. Legislation criminalising violence against women in the family is in place and the police now use female officers to interview rape victims, given the sensitivity required. All this advocacy work for gender equality and creating awareness of violence against women is not politically problematic. The government has been able to accommodate, even accept, AWARE's advocacy role and has made legislative and administrative changes accordingly. The next line of struggle is for criminalisation of rape by a spouse in a marriage, an issue that had already been debated in parliament but so far resisted by the government. AWARE has always been a liberal institution. While the government appears to grant legitimacy to AWARE's advocacy for gender equality, both the government and AWARE have undoubtedly upset conservatives who insist on "men at work and women at home" and who are unable to publicly voice their objections in the face of liberalising culture.

Beyond the relatively defensible advocacy for gender equality are other more thorny issues of sexuality. With new contraception and reproduction technologies, marriage, sexual activity and pregnancy has become three disparate activities rather than a constellation of connected activities within a moral universe of the family. One can be sexually active but not married; married but sexually inactive; married and sexually active without children; pregnant without husband and, ultimately, one could even be pregnant without sexual activity. Furthermore, with cultural liberalisation, sexuality is a matter of subjective choice and lifestyle, with polymorphous possibilities — lesbian, gay, bisexual, trans-sexual — switching from hetero to homo to bisexual, at will and desire. At its most liberal, sexuality is preferential rather than biological or psychologically determined.

As a liberal organisation, with English-educated professional women as the founding generation and ongoing membership, AWARE could hardly be expected to take a conservative position on sexuality. While it might not explicitly advocate gay liaisons it, nevertheless, has to be ideologically "pro-choice", of women's rights to their own bodies, which at its logical conclusion would include women's right to sexwork. It should not be surprising therefore that in its educational programmes, AWARE would not condemn lesbianism or homosexuality.

Cultural Conservatism and AWARE

In the face of the liberalising culture and the highly visible liberalisation of sexuality, cultural conservatives have been pushed progressively into the margins of public space and/or have retreated into the privacy of their own beliefs. Furthermore, the conservative-value-espousing government does not seem to be doing anything to stem the tide towards liberalisation; for example, the call to reexamine the abortion policy in view of the declining birth rates have fallen on deaf ears of the government; the proliferation of streetwalkers in Geylang seems to go without policing; on the cinema screen, sexuality gets increasingly explicit and teenage sexuality is on the rise. If the government were to remain inactive, it should be expected that some of the culturally conservative would do something about it, albeit this being Singapore it would not be vigilantes patrolling the streets.

Globally, concurrent with cultural liberalisation there has been an increase in membership in religious organisations, which should not be equated automatically with increased religiosity, as individuals are motivated by a multitude of reasons for joining religious organisations. For the same reason, increased membership should not be equated automatically with increased cultural conservatism or seen as a "backlash" against liberalising culture. Indeed, in the expanded religious community debates on sexuality rage on, with those who support gay and lesbian pastors and same-sex marriages to those who break away from "official" churches to maintain ideologically conservative resistance to changes in sexual practices and beliefs. Nevertheless, while it is possible to find the entire gamut of political ideological orientations among Christians, one would have to accept that the majority of the "born again" or evangelical new converts would be culturally conservative. Indeed, their conservatism may have driven them to the church rather than the church driving them to conservatism. The truth is likely to be a little bit of both. In Singapore, evangelical Christianity is one of the fastest expanding religions and is likely to have a greater share of the culturally conservative among the faithful.

The "taking over" of AWARE was executed by just such a group of culturally conservative women, who might have been motivated to do so because of the way they read their Christian scriptures and translated its teachings into anti-lesbian and anti-gay ideology. It was not a conspiracy of Christianity as a religion, as Christianity is by now a fragmented faith and institution. If there were a conspiracy, it was a conspiracy of one woman, the self-proclaimed "feminist mentor", Dr Thio Su Mien. Of the nine women who took over AWARE, six were later found to belong to the same church as Dr Thio, Church of Our Saviour. Obviously, beyond these six, other church members of similar ideological dispositions had been mobilised to quietly join AWARE and just as quietly come to the annual general meeting to vote in the six. The takeover was by a group of culturally conservative women who were Christians, even if their actions were motivated by their brand of Christianity.

In isolating the six individuals and Dr Thio, and treating the take-over of AWARE as their own initiative, misguided or otherwise, direct state intervention and potential criminalisation for disruption of religious harmony could be and had been avoided. The risk of state intervention was present when it was publicly known that Senior Pastor Derek Hong of the Church of Our Saviour had, from his Sunday pulpit, instructed his church members to go forth and support their "Christian sisters". At which point, the leaders of different religions and Christian denominations had to be mobilised to intervene and warned in unison against involving "religion" in the AWARE leadership contest. At which point, Pastor Hong admitted his mistake, apologised and withdrew his call for Christian unity. It was rumoured that the government had mobilised them behind the scenes; however, the Prime Minister, Lee Hsien Loong, clarified during his 2009 National Day Rally speech that he only spoke to the religious leaders after the event. The nine women who took over AWARE were left on their own.

Defined entirely as the act of a few women in their individual private capacity, there was no room and no need for direct state action. In spite of the call of some citizens, including *Straits Times* journalists, for the government to intervene, all its ministers would do were to give public "advice" about tolerance, maintaining civility and "live and let live". However, in doing so, it had the unintended consequence of furthering the liberalisation of culture; tolerance of difference being a foundational value of liberalism. In the end, the only act open to the government was to review and subsequently remove AWARE's curriculum from sexuality education in schools, which is entirely within the jurisdiction of the Ministry of Education.

Meanwhile, the rumoured bus-loads of Christians expected to come to support the culturally conservative new Exco did not materialise on the day of the EOGM. Instead, the team was left to face the groundswell of liberal Singaporeans, male and female, turning out to protect their own rights to belief, self-expression, self-formation and self-identity, regardless of whether they are sexually conservative or adventurous, hetero-normal or otherwise "queer"; queer being the hip-preferred self-address of those who are not hetero-normal. The result was a thorough routing of the conservatives. The liberals won the day.

The government shut out AWARE from schools and conservative education on sexuality was reinstated.

Conclusion

The AWARE saga is without doubt the triumph of the liberals over the conservative. However, it would be a mistake to conclude from this that Singapore has become overall a liberal society. One believes this to one's peril. The refrain that "Singaporeans are conservative" may remain true. Nevertheless, away from parliamentary political contest and religion and race in their public manifestations, the arena for public debates is framed by the liberal underpinnings of the national constitution which in guaranteeing the rights of individuals to beliefs and self-expression practically guarantees the liberalisation of culture, albeit heavily circumscribed by exigencies or expediencies of race and religion. Singapore seems destined to be settling down into an unchecked stranglehold on parliamentary power by the PAP which continues to manage the seemingly unstoppable unidirectional dynamic of a progressively liberalised cultural sphere, for some time in the future.

Note

1.   The press coverage and the various statements of the personalities and agencies surrounding the banning of the play have been collected in the inaugural issue of *Forum On Contemporary Art and Society* (FOCAS), published by The Necessary Stage, a theatre company that is active in social commentary through theatre. The substantive portion of this section draws heavily from these documents.

CHAPTER 2

Compensating for the Abdication of the Moral State?

Terence Chong

Introduction

One question looms unanswered in the aftermath of the AWARE (Association of Women for Action and Research) saga. Why did Christian conservatives feel the need to hijack a civil society organisation to push their agenda? This question is intriguing given the fact that society-state relations in Singapore, though heavily prescribed by the People's Action Party (PAP) state, have been far from static but, instead, have been dynamic and responsive to societal changes. After decades of industrialisation and economic growth, the broadening middle class has ushered in a more diverse identity politics and higher citizenry expectations with regard to the way in which politics is conducted, prompting the PAP state to embark on a trajectory of slogans from "civic society",[1] to "active citizenry"[2] to "public consultation"[3] when addressing society-state relations. This trajectory reflects not only the changing dynamics in society-state relations over the years but also the PAP state's ability to respond discursively to the socio-political circumstances of the day.

So what prompted a group of conservative Anglican Pentecostal Christians from the erstwhile little known Church of Our Saviour (COOS) to enter the arena of civil society to take over a women's rights group in a multicultural society where Christianity is well represented in the upper echelons of the professional world and local politics? Any serious attempt to answer the question needs to go beyond economic growth as the sole source of the PAP state's political legitimacy. It needs

25

to explore the ways in which the PAP state has often portrayed itself as highly moral, and how such portrayals have been politically useful in winning over moral conservatives, and why this changed.

The Morally Upright and Morally Conservative State

Moral politics in modern Singapore may be traced to the formation of the PAP, and argued to be the result of an English-educated bourgeois group struggling to bridge the cultural-economic gulf between itself and the Chinese-educated masses against the backdrop of communism in the late 1950s and early 1960s. Indeed, as a political party made up of middle class, overseas-educated and English-speaking Chinese that had no cultural ties to the working class Chinese-educated and dialect-speaking masses, the language of morals and morality served as a useful ideological bridge for the PAP.

After all, the Chinese-educated "held the English-educated in contempt for their lack of knowledge of Chinese culture and language, their 'commercial-mindedness', and their receptiveness to 'yellow culture' such as juke-boxes, Playboy magazines, sex films and dancing" (Yeo 1973: 177–8). Keenly sensitive to this perceived moral cleavage, the PAP embarked on an "anti-yellow culture" campaign in the 1960s to rid the consumer landscape of pornography, gambling and moral decadence. The PAP, in the effort to demonstrate its effectiveness upon taking charge of government, outlawed "pornography, striptease shows, pin-table saloons, even decadent songs" (Lee 1998: 326). More importantly, in the words of Lee Kuan Yew, such a move was useful for "outflanking the communists" which the PAP did with "puritanical zeal" (ibid.), and may be interpreted as an attempt by an English-educated middle class bourgeoisie to out-communist the communists in the morality stakes in order to win popular support.[4] Elsewhere, this political leveraging on morality by the PAP has been observed as the conscious construction of the "West" and the "Western Other" as a figure of excess and bodily indulgence, while presenting the "Asian" subject (as epitomised by the PAP) as the binary opposite (Yao 2007).

Since forming a government in 1959, the ruling party had always sought to portray itself as moral in two distinct ways. The first is as a *morally upright* state that did not tolerate corruption, nepotism or patronage. To this end, it has always emphasised high moral and ethical standards as criteria for politics and governance, and has brought into its fold those whom it considered were individuals of sound moral character. It is a socio-cultural system where the ideals of integrity, lawfulness, honesty and impartiality were accorded high levels of political capital. The morally upright state does not see itself as an entity that needs to seek these virtues for itself but instead, as an *a priori* embodiment of them, such that the task is not to attain integrity, but to preserve it. For the morally upright state, any erosion of its honesty and integrity would cause a corresponding erosion of its political capital, resulting in a loss of moral legitimacy. The second is as a *morally conservative* state that guarded the populace against the ills of pornography, liberal sexual attitudes, individualist lifestyle values and so on. Such a morally conservative state valued the ideals of cultural conservatism, dominant heterosexual values, traditional institutions like the nuclear family unit, and the generally patriarchal structures that delineate social norms. The morally conservative state is thus a trusted gatekeeper of its citizens, often seen as vulnerable and highly susceptible to external influence, regardless of the levels of education they enjoy, for it is a society-state relationship that is widely accepted to be openly asymmetrical in power and wisdom. With this dual discursive construction, along with competent governance and economic growth, the PAP has managed to generate a relationship of trust and political legitimacy between itself and the majority of citizens that has continuously returned the ruling party to power since 1959.

The PAP state's concern with the morality and morals of the nation only heightened with industrialisation. After years of economic growth and increasing evidence of mass consumerism, the ruling elite began to fear that the Chinese population was becoming too "Westernised" and at risk of "deculturalisation" (Goh 1978). Consequently, it has felt that existing civics and moral programmes were irrelevant to local students, paving the way for the implementation of the Religious Knowledge Studies syllabus in the early 1980s where the mainstream religions of Christianity, Islam, Buddhism, Hinduism and Confucian ethics for ethnic Chinese who professed neither Christianity nor Buddhism, were taught. This education policy conflated religion with morality, and was a radical state admission that religious instruction was central to moral education.

The moral state even found an embodied expression with its' rhetorical insistence that it was made up of the intellectual and moral elite, or in Confucian-speak, *junzhi* (honourable men) (*White Paper on Shared Values* 1991), and in Goh Chok Tong's public exaltation of Lee Kuan Yew as the "modern Confucius" (Kuo 1996). Other state discourses like the constant reminders to citizens to work hard, have respect for authority, privilege traditional definitions of the family, and to defer to paternalist structures have also added to the capital of the moralistic state; one which goes beyond the conventional state's duty to provide for its citizens' physical protection, but one which is also concerned for their moral and ethical well-being. These moral projects were an integral part of the nation-building process whereby the ruling elite sought to distinguish a culturally Asian society from the West, much like how one imagines oneself by imagining the Other. Although these moral projects were often linked to vague understandings of civilisational or ethnic culture that were never clearly defined, the underpinning values were distinctively patriarchal, politically and socially conservative, and enjoyed great nationalist currency when juxtaposed with Western concepts of liberalism or individualism.

The popular perception of the PAP government as a moral state has been vital to retaining the trust and confidence of conservative and religious segments of the population. Firstly, it served to demonstrate to the polity that it was able to balance the demands of economic pragmatism and capitalism with a conservative brand of morality and lifestyle values. This served to reassure many that regardless of the economic pressures (or temptations) faced by the city-state, it would always navigate its future with a socially conservative compass. Secondly, the trust that the moral conservatives had in the PAP state to do the "morally right" thing when it came to policy-decisions served an important political function in that it made religious-based political bargaining unnecessary. There was no compelling need for religious-based groups to mobilise themselves against a similarly morally conservative state. But perhaps most crucial of all, the PAP state was seen to take the initiative when it came to safeguarding the moral standards of society, and could be relied upon to uphold conservative brands of morality despite criticism, even ridicule, from more liberal voices, both domestic and international. This also played an important political role in that it acted as a buffer between sections of a middle class that had grown increasingly religious from the late 1970s onwards and a more liberal secular civil society. Many moral conservatives saw no need to move beyond traditional spaces such as churches, temples or mosques into civil society spaces to challenge public policies because the PAP state was trusted to be socially conservative. And because the PAP government had proven time and time again to be decisive and immune to criticism when implementing unpopular public policies, it was perceived that it would be equally steadfast in its moral convictions. All this changed in the last decade or so. Even as the PAP state remains steadfastly intolerant of corruption and other similar moral failings, a series of policy decisions heightened the perception that it was becoming less socially and morally conservative.

The End of the Moral State?

> Well, it's not a matter which I can decide or any government can decide. It's a question of what a society considers acceptable.[5]

Then Senior Minister Lee Kuan Yew's reply to a gay caller who asked if homosexuals had a future in Singapore during a CNN interview puts into sharp relief the altering state discourse on morality over the last decade. Lee's response was significant for two reasons. Firstly, and more obviously, it marked a relatively more liberal and informal attitude of the PAP government towards sex and sexual orientation. The ambition to become a global city has put the city-state in the global competition for global talent and capital. This competition has forced the government to reconcile local practices with international norms whether in the area of financial and commercial regulations or that of culture and entertainment where a more tolerant attitude towards liberal lifestyle values is the norm. The PAP government's efforts to reconcile the local with the global did not go unnoticed by the international media. *TIME* (30 June 2003) magazine observed that "As part of that effort, repressive government policies previously enforced in the name of social stability are being relaxed. The city now boasts seven saunas catering almost exclusively to gay clients, for example, something unthinkable even a few years ago."

Perhaps more disconcerting for the moral conservative was then Prime Minister Goh Chok Tong's revelation about gays in the civil service. According to the magazine, "Prime Minister Goh says his government now allows gay employees into its ranks, even in sensitive positions. The change in policy, inspired at least in part by the desire not to exclude talented foreigners who are gay, is being implemented without fanfare, Goh says, to avoid raising the hackles of more-conservative Singaporeans" (ibid.). Goh's remarks were also carried in the local press (*The Straits Times* 4 July 2003). For many moral conservatives, not only were societal values and morals sacrificed on the altar of economic growth and global city ambitions but, more fundamentally, the PAP state that they had come to rely on uphold conservative values changing from *within* into something they did not recognise.

Secondly, and just as important, Senior Minister Lee's remark that homosexuality and, by default, liberal lifestyle values, was "a question of what a society considers acceptable" indicated to many moral conservatives that the PAP state no longer desired to play a leading role when it came to issues of morality. Instead, it suggested that the government would increasingly look to society for cues and trends when it came to moral issues. This suggestion was reinforced by Prime Minister Lee Hsien Loong's speech in Parliament over the 377A debate in 2007. "When it comes to issues like the economy, technology, education, we better stay ahead of the game, watch where people are moving and adapt faster than others, ahead of the curve, leading the pack" but on issues of moral values "we will let others take the lead, we will stay one step behind the front line of change; watch how things work out elsewhere before we make any irrevocable moves" (Lee 2007). No longer willing to take the moral initiative as it did in the past — or, as PM Lee noted, "when western countries went for experimental life-styles in the 1960s — the hippies, free love, all the rage, we tried to keep it out" (ibid.) — the government today has clearly adopted a less puritan, even more consultative approach towards issues of moral values. This shift in approach may have given rise to the perception amongst many moral conservatives that the state had abdicated its role as moral guardian of society.

A host of other major public policy decisions and high profile events seemed to support this perception. One highly visible example of increasing moral latitude for many conservatives was in the area of film censorship. There is little doubt that greater levels of graphic sex, violence and alternative sexuality had found their way to local screens thanks to the steady relaxation of censorship throughout the 1990s, beginning with the 1992 *Censorship Review Committee Report*. There was also strong resistance, for example, when it was announced in late 2004 that two casinos would accompany the two Integrated Resorts in Marina Bay and Sentosa. Many morally-conservative Singaporeans voiced their disapproval, many starting petitions, while the National Council of Churches of Singapore made clear that it opposed the casinos (*The Straits Times* 30 Dec. 2004). The now-defunct *Crazy Horse* topless Parisian cabaret show also aroused great consternation from the moral conservatives. According to Lee Kuan Yew, when the cabinet was debating the cabaret, several ministers were against the idea. As such

"He said to his colleagues: Let the show in. It does not make sense to keep things out in this globalised age" (*The Straits Times* 23 April 2007). The papers went on to quote him as saying:

> "Look, once upon a time, Singaporeans watched peep shows. You know, you pay 10 cents and you turn an old film in a box at Chinese wayangs. Today, they are going to Paris, they go to the *Folies Bergère*. I mean it doesn't make sense anymore," he said, referring to the renowned topless cabaret show. I said, "Let it go". So they said, "No, we must stop this, stop that". I said, "You either go with the world and be part of the world, or you will find that we become a quaint, a quixotic, esoteric appendage of the world." (ibid.)

Not only was this a sharp contrast to the "anti-yellow culture" campaign of the 1960s, it also suggested to moral conservatives that changing economic realities and globalisation had rendered timeless moral values "quaint" and "quixotic". Such a pragmatic interpretation immediately found itself at odds with the supposedly eternal and unchanging relevance of religious teachings and moral values. Many had found comfort and security in the water-tight dichotomy between morality and pragmatism, timelessness and modernity, eternal values and evolutionary change, and it now seemed as though there was more porosity than ever before.

Nevertheless, for many moral conservatives, the trend was clear: the PAP state, pressured to deliver economic growth, was becoming more tolerant of liberal lifestyle values and amenable to morally questionable policy decisions. There was also some suggestion that religious conservatives within the Cabinet were perturbed enough with certain political decisions to resign.[6] In the belief that the PAP leadership now prefers to follow when it comes to moral issues and looks to society for the moral pulse of the nation, both moral conservatives and liberals alike have sought increasingly to make themselves heard in the hopes of swaying public discourse and policy decisions. In fact, one of the many clarion calls throughout the AWARE saga when moral conservatives and liberals were mobilising support was the "need to make our voices heard" (*The Straits Times* 5 May 2009) such that previously accepted concepts of the "civic society" or "public consultation" may no longer be adequate to accommodate the emerging contours of cultural forces and identity politics that are setting the scene for a more confrontational and uncompromising inter-NGO as well as society-state relations.

Civil Society Spaces and the Struggle to Make Moral Claims

The takeover of AWARE by Christian women should be seen as an initiative by moral conservatives to fill the vacuum left by the morally conservative state. Prompted by a combination of moral panic over the perceived promotion of homosexuality and lesbianism, and the fear that unless they stake their claim and articulate their interests, they would be overwhelmed by sexually liberal voices, these conservative Christian women entered the civil society sphere to re-make a secular NGO in their own image. Such initiatives, however, should not be seen as a coherent strategy from what is in fact a heterogeneous Christian community where a wide spectrum of political and cultural values may be found. Instead, in this particular case, COOS was an aggressive vehicle for a body of conservative lifestyle values and beliefs which, in reality, cuts across religion and race. For example, Thio Su Mien's complaint that AWARE's sex education syllabus, under the Ministry of Education's (MOE) Comprehensive Sex Education (CSE) programme, had encouraged local students to see homosexuality in "neutral" terms instead of "negatively", struck a chord with Christians and non-Christians alike. In the absence of the morally conservative state, moral conservatives took it upon themselves to become more watchful and vigilant over the moral health of the nation, and were less willing to compromise when "vulnerable" citizens, in this case, secondary school students, were at stake. On one hand, moral conservatives believe that the burden is now on them to maintain the moral standards of society, while on the other, liberals see the opportunity to highlight patriarchal or discriminatory areas in public policies, thus leading to a whistle-blowing culture on both sides of the moral divide. As such, civil society will see an increase not just in religious fervour but also a clash of identity politics and worldviews that are informed as much by religious doctrines as they are by liberal ideologies. The end result is a civil society that will see a more intense struggle between religious conservatives and liberals over the right to define the moral values of the nation.

Some of these struggles will most certainly emerge around traditional "hot button" issues like abortion, homosexuality, euthanasia, stem-cell research and censorship. In fact the issue of euthanasia was starved of public debate by the AWARE saga. The Singapore police denied pro-euthanasia group EXIT International a permit to hold a talk scheduled at the National Library at Victoria Street on 13 May 2009. This was even though the head of the group, Dr Philip Nitschke, was told by the Ministry of Manpower that he did not need a special work pass to come and that 28 people had already signed for the talk (*The Straits Times* 1 May 2009). The ban on the euthanasia seminar was all the more puzzling given that the Health Minister, Khaw Boon Wan, had openly asked if Singapore needed to reconsider its laws on euthanasia given its rapidly aging population, with clear hints that a public debate on the matter would be welcome by the government (*The Straits Times* 30 Oct. 2008). These conflicting signals from the government are best seen as an exercise in damage control. Coming in the midst of the AWARE saga, the government opted for the more politically expedient choice of banning the euthanasia talk in case religious and moral conservatives became more agitated than they already were. Here, it may be argued that even though the PAP state relinquishes its moralistic role, it continues to exert its authority to manage moral debate.

Finally, the AWARE saga offers one noteworthy observation for local civil society and middle class politics. Despite the many times derogatory, sometimes extremist, statements were made by moral conservatives about homosexuals, the mode of resistance and activism was resolutely civic and legal. The AWARE takeover was, for better or worse, entirely through democratic and constitutional means. Meanwhile, the middle class educational competence has also resulted in the corporatisation of activism. A case in point is the strongly Christian-influenced group Focus on the Family and its corporate ties with DBS Bank as the latter's charity of choice. This corporate tie-up, overseen by Josie Lau, was discontinued after public protest. Such modes of activism which utilise civic avenues, constitutional means, or corporate tie-ups will only grow as middle class activists become better informed and better educated. In addition to conventional tactics such as petitions or traditional fund-raising, they will adopt the vocabulary of capitalism and corporate-speak to expand their networks and influence. All this is symptomatic of an increasingly educated middle class within which certain groups are now using its cultural capital and professional competence to struggle more covertly for their own interests.

Conclusion

It would be impossible for the PAP state to return to moral conservatism of the 1950s and 1960s. One of the criteria for global city status seems to be political and social tolerance, if not embrace, of diverse brands of morality, lifestyle values and ideologies. Unlike in the earlier phase of its economic development which focused on manufacturing industries, Singapore now has its sights set on being a hub for higher-value activities such as research and development, the creative and media industries, in addition to banking and finance. Where it was once plausible for a culturally and morally conservative space to be economically vibrant because of the type of industries it attracted, the desire for higher-value activities that require the creativity and intellect of highly professional and skilled talent now demand a more liberal and tolerant space to live and work in. Reading these trends well are both moral conservatives and liberals who have a stake in shaping local spaces and discourses to their own image. The result will be more frequent struggles and conflict to determine the morality of the nation.

Notes

1. The term "civic society" is one of the PAP state's earlier expressions of "civil society" and is generally understood as an ideological attempt to describe a Singapore civil society as one that is non-confrontational, apolitical and concerned with welfare issues such as care for the elderly or under-privileged. It is one where NGOs serve as an unproblematic bridge between the state's interests and the needs of society (Yeo 1991).

2. In 1999 the Singapore 21 Committee published its report which called for "active citizenry" as part of the country's efforts towards nation-building. "Active citizenry", for the committee, connoted greater civic participation and sense of belonging.

3. "Public consultation" was a key idea in the Singapore 21 exercise which saw government representatives tap the ideas and views of ordinary citizens with regard to aspirations and visions for the country.

4. This is not to suggest that the complex relationship between the PAP and the Chinese-speaking masses may be reduced to the moral-social contract between two cultural-linguistic groups. Indeed the forces of anti-colonialism and the ability of the PAP to win the emotional and intellectual argument for merger with Malaysia in 1963 were crucial to the relationship. Nevertheless, the socio-cultural divide cannot be ignored.

5. Quoted from yawningbread.org <http://www.yawningbread.org/arch_1998/yax-127.htm> [accessed 31 July 2009].

6. Senior Minister Goh Chok Tong revealed that one key reason for S. Dhanabalan's resignation from Cabinet in 1992 was the latter's displeasure with the way in which the government had dealt with the so-called "Marxist conspiracy" in 1987. SM Goh was quoted as saying: "At that time, given the information, he was not fully comfortable with the action we took.... His make-up is that of a very strong Christian so he felt uncomfortable

and thought there could be more of such episodes in future … he'd better leave the Cabinet. I respected him for his view" (*The Straits Times* 6 Sept. 2009).

References

Goh, Keng Swee, 1978, *Report on the Ministry of Education*. Singapore: Ministry of Education.

Kuo, Eddie, 1996, "Confucianism as Political Discourse in Singapore: The Case of an Incomplete Revitalisation Movement", in *Confucian Traditions in East Asian Modernity: Moral Education and Economic Culture in Japan and the Four Mini-Dragons*, ed. Tu Weiming. Massachusetts: Harvard University Press.

Lee Hsien Loong, 2007, Parliamentary Speech on Section 377A (23 October). Singapore: Hansard.

Lee Kuan Yew, 1998, *The Singapore Story*. Singapore: Times Edition.

The Straits Times, 4 July 2003, "Govt more open to employing gays now", by M. Nirmala.

————, 30 Dec. 2004, "Views split over proposed safeguards", by Kelvin Wong and Glenys Sim.

————, 23 April 2007, "Adjusting to the realities of a globalising world", by Peh Shing Huei.

————, 30 Oct. 2008, "Red-ink euthanasia letter 'conveyed reader's pain'", by Tan Hui Yee.

————, 1 May 2009, "No go for talk by 'Dr Death'", by Sandra Davie.

————, 5 May 2009, Online discussion board <http://comment.straitstimes.com/showthread.php?t=19648&page=2> [accessed 3 Aug. 2009].

————, 6 Sept. 2009, "Why Dhana left Cabinet in 1992".

TIME, 30 June 2003, "The Lion in Winter", by Simon Elegant.

White Paper on Shared Values, 1991. Singapore: Ministry of Information, Communication and the Arts.

Yao Souchou, 2007, *Singapore: The State and the Culture of Excess*. London: Routledge.

Yeo Kim Wah, 1973, *Political Development in Singapore 1945–55*. Singapore: Singapore University Press.

Yeo, George, 1991, "Civic Society — Between the Family and the State", Inaugural NUSS Lecture, 20 June, World Trade Centre Auditorium, Singapore.

CHAPTER 3

Not Quite Shutting Up and Sitting Down: The Singapore Government's Role in the AWARE Saga

Azhar Ghani and Gillian Koh

Introduction

An internal matter. Not a "national issue"; a "domestic dispute" even (*The Straits Times* 20 April 2009; 25 April 2009). Early descriptions of the leadership tussle at the Association of Women for Action and Research (AWARE) by politicians and media pundits alike clearly indicated that they did not think much of it at the time. Yet, after five weeks, it became the topic that months later, many were hoping the Prime Minister would address in the most important speech in Singapore's political calendar.[1]

Before the saga was highlighted by Prime Minister Lee Hsien Loong in his National Day Rally speech on 16 August 2009, other government leaders had already signposted its importance. Their concerns centred on the role played by religion — in this case, Christian opposition to homosexuality, as acted upon by a group associated with Josie Lau that eventually took over AWARE's executive committee (Exco) after its March elections. Religion and homosexuality can become a particularly volatile mix, given that the acceptance of homosexuality is a value-based decision that could be informed by one's religion, or deeply held moral and political inclinations. The robust parliamentary debate in

2007 over a parliamentary petition to repeal Section 377A of the Penal Code, thereby legalising homosexual acts, and the public debate outside the House, were a clear testament to the potential of this issue to polarise society even when there had not been any overt references to religion. This could only be exacerbated if the impression, whether formed by media reports or from other sources, founded or unfounded, was that one side in the saga had been motivated by their religious conviction to take over an established secular organisation to change its agenda on homosexuality.

Keeping "religion" and "politics" separate is a key rule of political engagement in Singapore. In a speech after the resolution of the saga, Nominated Member of Parliament Thio Li-Ann argued that despite the rule, the Singapore model of secularism was not anti-religious and that religion had been allowed to play a role in public debate (Thio 2009). Indeed, in the past, leaders of religious umbrella groups had made the views of their respective faith communities known to the government and the public through statements and letters on issues of gambling, censorship and bioethics. In all these cases, there was overt association of the advocacy on the issues with religious values.

This role of religion is, however, circumscribed by the Maintenance of Religious Harmony Act (MRHA),[2] the Sedition Act,[3] the Internal Security Act (ISA), and parts of the Penal Code,[4] and supplemented by informal rules of political regulation that we have come to know as OB (out-of-bound) markers. To understand this framework of rules, one has to look back on the so-called Marxist Conspiracy of 1987, which resulted in the MRHA being formulated in 1990. In the 1987 incident, a total of 22 individuals were detained under the Internal Security Act (ISA) for what the government believed to be attempts to subvert existing social and political order, and to establish a Marxist state. The Internal Security Department (ISD) said the case demonstrated how religion could be used for subversive purposes. Those detained either worked full time or volunteered in Catholic Church-affiliated organisations that dealt with the rights and welfare of workers, both local and foreign.

The White Paper on the Maintenance of Religious Harmony Bill which was tabled in Parliament in December 1989 provided key references for what the government would accept as the role of religion in public debate. It referred to the President's Address at the opening of Parliament on 9 January 1989 that "religion must be kept rigorously separate from politics, [for] in a multi-religious society, if one group violates this taboo, others will follow suit, and the outcome will be militancy and conflict". In addition, it detailed the government's position on religion and politics, that Singapore "must be a strictly secular state [where] … the government must claim ultimate political authority from the Constitution, and not from any divine or ecclesiastical sanction". The government "must remain neutral in its relations with the different religious groups, not favouring any of them in preference to the others. [The government's] duty [is thus] to ensure that every citizen is free to choose his own religion, and that no citizen, in exercising his religious or other rights infringes upon the rights and sensitivities of other citizens" (White Paper on the Maintenance of Religious Harmony 1989).

The Takeover

Where then, do we place the AWARE saga? How should we understand it given the government's record of dealing with the nexus of religious groups and civil society on issues of great public interest? To this day, those from the so-called "new guard" led by Lau and its supporters maintain that religion was not an issue in the AWARE saga but morality. According to Dr Thio Su Mien, it was the media that painted it as such, suggesting that those covering the developments were biased or pro-homosexual (Personal interview 5 Aug. 2009). They believe the new guard sought to champion a broad-based rejection of homosexuality that was in line with government policy and public morality. More specifically, they wished to block a perceived strategy emanating from AWARE aimed at desensitising and creating acceptance for the lifestyle among the young — an impression that members of the so-called "old guard" of long-time AWARE activists have since refuted (*The Straits Times* 25 April 2009).

This agenda against the mainstreaming of the homosexual lifestyle was confirmed by Thio who identified herself as the link among six of the eight new guard Exco members and someone who had shared with them concerns over what she saw as AWARE's pro-gay leanings (Personal interview 5 Aug. 2009). While the group had joined AWARE to also "organise activities whereby they can put to use their talents to teach, mentor, and train others in the areas that they have expertise", its motivation was "*first*, to steer [AWARE] away from the homosexual agenda" (Email reply to authors 16 Aug. 2009). Indeed, although the group did not plan to take over AWARE, it did want to be in a position to influence its programmes; or as Thio said "it was hoped that many [would] turn up and many [would] be voted in" (ibid.).

From the new guard's perspective, it was doing a public good by stepping up for the majority of Singaporeans whose values, whether religiously-informed or otherwise, could be undermined if any segment, especially civil society activists from a trusted, well-regarded non-government organisation such as AWARE, were to promote the homosexual lifestyle as being "normal".[5] From this perspective, no ill-will of the sort covered by the quartet of religious harmony-related legislation (MRHA, Sedition Act, ISA and Penal Code) would be sowed among religious groups, and there would be no reason for the government to intervene.

The government, on the other hand, received feedback to suggest otherwise. In his post-mortem of the saga on 15 May, Deputy Prime Minister and Minister of Home Affairs Wong Kan Seng said that the government was worried about "the disquieting public perception" over the AWARE takeover (Wong 2009). In his National Day Rally Speech, the Prime Minister explicitly stated that it was the government's own view that religious activism had been at play: "[W]hat worried us was that this was an attempt by a religiously motivated group who shared a strong religious fervour to enter civil space, take over an NGO it disapproved of, and impose their agenda." He said the saga not only "risked a broader spillover into relations between different religions", but had also made many Singaporeans, including many Christians, worried. In the end, the government agreed with the media portrayal of the saga as a coup that was objectionable for the hidden agenda that was at play, and for the precedent it might set for how other religious communities might relate to civil society organisations and public advocacy.

Yet, despite this perspective and the government's record of intervention on religion-related problems, Prime Minister Lee said in the same speech that the government had "stayed out of this", and only spoke to the religious leaders "first the Christians and then the religious leaders of all faiths" after the "dust had settled" (Lee 2009). Going by what is publicly known, the government did stay its hand even as events unfolded, and allowed AWARE members to deal with the tussle according to the organisation's rules. The only explicit intervention came when the Singapore Police Force vetoed the choice of Singapore Expo (a large venue for exhibitions and events) in Changi as the venue for the 2 May Extraordinary General Meeting (EGM) where a vote of no confidence against the new guard Exco was to be called. The police said the step was taken due to the "strong possibility that a coming together of members and supporters of the opposing camps at the same venue may result in law and order problems. There have been reports of death threats, intimidation and harassment over the last two weeks. There are also reports that both groups are mobilizing their supporters for the meetings" (*The Straits Times* 30 April 2009). At that time, there was a growing online buzz that the EGM would coincide with a large Christian conference at the Singapore Expo.

Indeed, the government appeared to have maintained distance from the saga despite indirect attempts to draw it into the controversy. Former AWARE president Braema Mathi, a member of the old guard, said in an interview that those from her camp had been "informally offering feedback and insights on the saga to Members of Parliament and ministers they met" (Personal interview 28 Aug. 2009). As long-time civil society activists, many of them were known to, and knew, government leaders. Mathi, a former Nominated Member of Parliament herself, said however, that she did not know what impact these informal outreach efforts had (ibid.).

When the media began to focus on the new guard's anti-homosexuality position, Thio identified AWARE's Comprehensive Sexuality Education (CSE) programme for schools as a key factor that motivated the new guard and its supporters to join AWARE and influence the organisation (*The Straits Times* 24 April 2009). The programme had elements in the trainers' guide that suggested that homosexuality was "perfectly normal" — a fact then unknown to the Ministry of Education (MOE) (*The Straits Times* 22 May 2009). Thio said these elements were a source of negative feedback from parents. As the CSE issue involved schools under the purview of MOE, the door was open for the government to play a more active role in the saga. MOE addressed the concerns by noting then that it had received no such feedback on the programme (*The Straits Times* 29 April 2009) and then stayed out of the "local" tangle.

Interestingly, the CSE programme became a real issue *only after* the new guard was in leadership and had access to internal documents related to the programme.[6] Instead, the initial concern about AWARE's alleged pro-gay leanings stemmed from the screening of a film celebrating lesbian love at an AWARE charity premiere in 2007, and AWARE's defence of the film choice in response to public disquiet. Equally interesting was the fact that MOE began receiving the negative feedback from parents *only after* the Ministry had publicly refuted Thio's earlier claims that parents had been unhappy with the AWARE programme (*The Straits Times* 1 May 2009a). Unlike the AWARE new guard which had gained access to internal documents related to the association's CSE programme, MOE did not know till much later that these materials contained messages on homosexuality deemed inappropriate. Having found out the full facts, MOE did what it had to do on 6 May — four days after the EGM — and suspended the programme (*The Straits Times* 7 May 2009), perhaps with as little hesitation as it had dismissed the new guard's concerns earlier. Throughout its handling of the matter, there was a palpable sense that while MOE strove to ensure its policies were not compromised, it was also consciously treading the middle ground between the opposing groups. It was only later that Education Minister Ng Eng Hen would chastise both sides for "drag[ging] [schools] into this melée" (*The Straits Times* 22 May 2009). This reflected the government's deliberate posture of ensuring that it would "not be misunderstood as taking sides" before the EGM (Wong 2009), as any action that MOE took could be read as tacit approval or disapproval of the actions and positions taken by the two sides. In this particular episode, the balancing act was made easier, given how the two opposing parties conducted themselves. The new guard played by the rules, and employed the politically-acceptable and polite avenue of petitioning for change. Likewise, the old guard of AWARE did not protest when its programme was pulled out from schools. Instead, its response was one of resigned acceptance and, significantly, it also avoided blaming the government.

Religion, Civil Society and Schools: Two Contrasting Cases

Contrast this to a previous controversy involving religion, civil society and schools that arose in 2002, and again in 2003, that had been noted for the strong government reaction it provoked. This was when a total of five Muslim primary school girls were suspended from classes when their parents insisted they wear the *tudung* (headscarf) to school. In both the *tudung* controversy and the AWARE episode, groups of Singaporeans ventured into what is known as the "common space"[7] (schools in the case of the *tudung* episode; and secular civic group and, later, schools in the AWARE saga), and acted in ways deemed to be motivated by their religious values. In the case of the *tudung* episode, the Prime Minister, Deputy Prime Minister, Education Minister and Minister-in-charge of Muslim Affairs all weighed in with strong comments (*The Straits Times* 28 Jan. 2002). Action was also taken — opposition politician Chee Soon Juan, who showed his support for the girls by addressing the issue at Speakers' Corner, was fined under the Public Entertainment Exemption Order (*Channel News Asia* 30 July 2003), while a Malaysian lawyer who had offered to provide the girls' parents with *pro bono* legal service to challenge the "no-*tudung*" ruling in Singapore's courts was denied an employment pass by the Manpower Ministry (*The Straits Times* 13 Sept. 2002). There were probably many reasons for the different approach, but in comparison with the AWARE saga, there were several distinguishing points.

First was the challenge to a long-standing rule — in this case, MOE's "no-*tudung*" rule — instigated by a protagonist who had been a gadfly to the government on several issues relating to the Muslim community in the past, namely Zulfikar Shariff, who was the chief executive officer of a civics group known as Fateha. Second was the politicisation of the issue by the Singapore Democratic Party's Chee. Third, the controversy had involved Malaysian politicians. The lawyer who had offered his services was from the Democratic Action Party. Members from the Islamic Parti Islam SeMalaysia (PAS) visited the families of the affected girls in a show of support at Zulfikar's invitation (*The Straits Times* 26 May 2002). These were particularly provocative actions. They sought to undermine the authority of the Singapore government and the local Malay-Muslim leadership which works within the corporatist framework of the government. Finally, the government viewed the controversy as one where an assertion of separate identities could come at the expense of the common space shared by all Singaporeans (*The Straits Times* 9 Feb. 2002). On the other hand, the evidence points to the government exercising considerable restraint during the AWARE saga. One reason for the measured response was that it was probably bound by the need to demonstrate a neutral stance on NGO politics. In public pronouncements later, this neutral stance would be expressed as the government being less concerned over who would control AWARE, since the outcome would not influence its long-held carefully calibrated position on homosexuality.

Another reason was how the protagonists conducted themselves. There may have been death threats and intimidating remarks made on the Internet against members of the new guard; there may have been demeaning descriptions of homosexuals from the new guard's camp and its supporters;[8] there was even a rowdy EGM to cap it all off. However, in the end, we saw the culmination of how both sides tried to abide by AWARE's constitution and keep the conflict "local"; and they did not, ostensibly, seek to mobilise the political opposition, or appeal to foreign parties. What did happen however was a mobilisation of religious followers on behalf of the new guard, which appeared to be when the line was crossed.[9]

Crossing the Line and the Government's "Under-the-Radar" Intervention

However, as Prime Minister Lee observed in his National Day Rally speech, there were other ways of intervening away from the public eye, and this was how the government chose to act in this case. What the public saw was the chairman of the National Council of Churches Singapore (NCCS), Archbishop Dr John Chew, making what is now widely seen and commended as a timely and pivotal intervention — Archbishop Chew's statement of 30 April stating that the NCCS did not condone churches getting involved in the saga or for pulpits to be used to mobilise support for secular organisations (*The Straits Times* 1 May 2009b). While it had been portrayed as an instance of self-regulation by the leader of the religious community involved, there was much more to it.

The statement came soon after an eyebrow-raising sermon by a priest from the Church of Our Saviour, where six of the new guard Exco and Thio worship. Senior Pastor Derek Hong's sermon was intended for his own flock but reported on by the Internet-based citizen journalism site, *The Online Citizen* (27 April 2009). In his sermon, Hong had urged the women in his flock to be engaged and support Lau and "her sisters" at AWARE. More pertinently, he had invoked religion in a reference to homosexuality, when he said that while a show of support was "not a crusade against the people", it had to be done because "there's a line that God has drawn for us, and we don't want our nation crossing that line". This was probably the game-changer. By invoking God and urging for support for the new guard from the pulpit, Hong cemented the view that religion was the central issue in the saga. Our interviews suggest that it was at this point that the government decided it had to intervene. The government's rationale was that to allow a crossing over of religion into secular space in this instance would set a precedent for other faith groups to do likewise, perhaps not on this issue, but others in the future.

Significantly, the MRHA was not invoked. Instead, there were under-the-radar conversations between the ISD and Hong, the Archbishop, leaders of other Christian churches, and heads of other religious groups.[10] Archbishop Chew described the ISD contact as bearing "no directives from the government". He said: "They said, 'Oh, how is the Church coming in to help in this situation?' It was more of a sharing of concerns. I think it would be necessary and appropriate in certain situations for the government to do just that" (Personal interview 5 Aug. 2009). What the ISD intervention did was to prevent a mobilisation, not by the churches, but by church members who had rallied support for the new guard by getting their friends to sign up as AWARE members ahead of the EGM. The government-prompted NCCS statement, and its endorsement by the government, might have persuaded close to 1,000 of these supporters — based on Josie Lau's estimates (Personal interview 10 Aug. 2009) — that it would be wise not to attend the EGM. Even those who did chose not to speak up. This changed the tone of the proceedings and outcome of the EGM.

To learn that the ISD had contacted the religious leaders was not a surprise. What might surprise some, though, would be why the ISD decided not to meet the two opposing parties in the saga to let them know of the heated situation and call for a cooling-off. One possible explanation is that, by approaching only the religious leaders, the ISD managed to exercise enough influence over the bigger environment to contain the situation, and yet still stay out of the ring. Arguably, this prevented the dispute from spiraling into either a larger struggle between religious conservatives and liberals, or a contest for space among the different religious groups. Whether the government would have maintained the peripheral mode of intervention had things continued to heat up is not clear. What is clear is that the government would be willing to adopt a light touch and not jump to direct intervention at the first sign of trouble. It would make the pre-emptive behind-the-scenes strike if religion were perceived to be involved in political mobilisation. This *laissez-faire* approach to let civil society look after its own affairs sits nicely with the government's stated aim of encouraging more active civic participation.

Given its view that the media coverage had "amplif[ied]" the situation (Lee 2009), it was not surprising to hear that the government had been in touch with members of the Singapore media to express its concerns on the reportage. Without providing details, Minister for Information, Communications and the Arts Lui Tuck Yew was quoted as saying in September 2009 that he had contacted media editors regarding their coverage (*The Straits Times* 10 Sept. 2009). Given the power of the media to influence public perception, understanding the specifics of the "contact" would provide a fuller picture of how the saga played out. Details on what transpired in these "contacts" are not known, so it is not clear if they had much of an impact, if any at all. However, in our analysis, there appeared to be no change in the tone of the coverage up to the EGM.

Conclusion

In conclusion, whatever course of action that the government decided on during the saga, it reiterated the following principles relating to the governance of religious peace in Singapore (Lee 2009). First, all religious groups have to exercise tolerance and restraint, and not expect Singapore's societal mores to conform to all the rules of their individual religions. Hence, any attempt by religious or religiously-motivated groups to promote their beliefs — even if they were commonly held by the majority — in the public sphere, could breach the OB markers since no single group should be allowed to have such power. Second, religion must be kept separate from all politics, not just party politics, because if "one group invokes religion this way, other groups are bound to say 'I also need powerful support'" and push back (ibid.). This would include politics with a small 'p', which covers grassroots activism. Third, the government has to remain secular, neutral and fair because it "hold[s] the ring so that all groups can practise their faiths freely without colliding with one another in Singapore" (ibid.). And finally, the common space among Singaporeans must be maintained, and kept neutral and secular because "that's the only way all of us can feel at home in Singapore and at ease" (ibid.).

Had the new guard understood these principles, the AWARE saga might not have happened, or would have turned out differently. The new guard probably believed that it had the approval of the conservative majority, especially those of other religious denominations that would not approve of homosexuality. With mass support, the likelihood of getting the government's support, they thought, should also increase as the government had previously made it clear that it will go with the majority view on issues of public morality. However, instead of seeing the new guard as a group that was championing a common interest, many Singaporeans probably saw the group's move as a unilateral encroachment by a bunch of conservative Christians into what is supposed to be a neutral common space — never mind the fact that many of them probably cared little for AWARE as an organisation, even if they did share its values of inclusiveness, tolerance and diversity. Certainly, the old guard ensured that Singaporeans would not miss that point — as *The Straits Times* columnist Paul Jacob observed, "the team ousted from power [...] dug up statements that some in the new team made publicly and in their *personal capacity* about issues such as homosexuality" (*The Straits Times* 20 April 2009) — before the view that conservative Christianity had a central role in the agenda of the new guard was finally cemented in the public mind by Hong's sermon.

What those in the new guard had not anticipated was that the government would be more worried about the public disquiet over the AWARE takeover than by any suggestion that AWARE had been hijacked by a homosexual agenda and needed to be saved. Here, the government applied what appears to be a firm belief that the peace one sees on the surface of Singapore's multi-racial and multi-religious milieu is not due to an absence of tension. Rather, it is the result of constant tension between groups whose private spaces abut not just one another, but also neutral, common spaces such as the civic space occupied by groups like AWARE.

In this state of constant tension, equilibrium is maintained by Singapore's framework of laws and OB markers. A push for more space or influence by any group, whether perceived or real, would result in a push-back by the others, whether on the same issue or on other issues in future. Hence, resolution and peace are never spoken of as an elimination of "the other", but a recognition that there are entrenched, deeply-held positions on the issues and that each group is to respect the *status quo* and not seek pre-eminence. In this state of tension, the government's role as arbiter could be undermined if it is seen to endorse moves that give any group a perceived unfair opportunity at resetting the equilibrium by claiming more space for itself. Anyone venturing into civic space with a religious motivation would do well to remember this.

Notes

1. In his 2009 National Day Rally speech the Prime Minister had described the saga as "one recent issue, which I am sure you have been waiting for me to talk about", a description affirmed by the audience at the Rally with an audible response.

2. Under the MRHA, members of any religious group would be issued restraining orders by the Minister of Home Affairs if he is satisfied that the person has committed any of the following acts: (a) causing feelings of enmity, hatred, ill-will or hostility between different religious groups; (b) carrying out activities to promote a political cause, or a cause of any political party while, or under the guise of, propagating or practising any religious belief; (c) carrying out subversive activities under the guise of propagating or practising any religious belief; or (d) exciting disaffection against the President or the Government while, or under the guise of, propagating or practising any religious belief.

3. Section 3(e) of the Sedition Act defines seditious tendency as a tendency to promote feelings of ill-will and hostility between different races or classes of the population of Singapore.

4. Chapter XV of the Penal Code covers offences relating to religion or race. Section 398A under this chapter states that whoever (a) by words, either spoken or written, or by signs or by visible representations or otherwise, knowingly promotes or attempts to promote, on grounds of religion or race, disharmony or feelings of enmity, hatred or ill-will between different religious or racial groups; or (b) commits any act which he knows is prejudicial to the maintenance of harmony between different religious or racial groups and which disturbs or is likely to disturb the public tranquility, shall be punished with imprisonment for a term which may extend to three years, or with fine, or both.

5. Whether the values of the conservative majority in Singapore could be undermined by an allegedly pro-gay AWARE appears debatable, given the association's apparent wane at that time, as reflected in its dwindling membership which stood at an all time low just before the saga began. In interviews with both Thio Su Mien and Josie Lau, they did not make it clear whether they actually saw AWARE as a pivotal arena in the values contest. Neither did they explain why members of the new guard felt compelled to head off the alleged homosexual agenda in AWARE, as opposed to the non-confrontational option of using other platforms or avenues to campaign for the values that they believe in.

6. In the interview with Thio (5 Aug. 2009), the question was asked "So was it because the team had gone into Aware that they were able to get hold of this material?". Thio replied "Yes. But they were not going in just looking for that, they were going to do other things. The pressure was such that, I

mean, one of these women said, I think maybe we should go and look at it …."

7. During the 2002 *tudung* controversy, the Singapore government introduced the concept of "common space" in the discourse of race relations in Singapore (*The Straits Times* 2 Feb. 2002). In a letter to *The Straits Times*, Lim Chee Hwee, Press Secretary to the Education Minister wrote: "We can view Singapore society as being represented by four overlapping circles, each representing one of the major ethnic groups. Within this overlap area, there is national treatment for all, be it opportunities for higher education or access to health-care services. Each community, however, retains the freedom to practise its own religion and customs. This is represented by the space outside of the overlap area … Singaporeans should cherish the common space that we have and strive to preserve it rather than acceding to requests by each community or group within a community to seek to expand its space at the expense of the common area."

    Before the concept of "common space" entered the discourse, the old inter-religious and inter-ethnic relations paradigm had stressed the imperative of not encroaching into the spaces of others, as seen in how aggressive proselytisation by certain groups to win converts was cited as a concern that led to the introduction of the Maintenance of Religious Harmony Act (*The Straits Times* 24 Feb. 1990).

8. At the new guard press conference, several members of the Exco, including its president Josie Lau, detailed the kind of harassment that they had to deal with since the saga went public (*The Straits Times* 24 April 2009b). At the same press conference, Thio described lesbians as being "in pain". She said: "(They are) very often from families where you have abusive fathers, they do things with their daughters and the daughters revolt, rebel against society." Later, she described lesbians as "sexually challenged women" (*The Straits Times* 18 May 2009).

9. This can be inferred from Deputy Prime Minister and Home Affairs Minister Wong Kan Seng's press statement on 15 May 2009 (Wong 2009). Warning that the government "will not stand by and watch when intemperate activism threatens our social fabric", he said: "If religious groups start to campaign to change certain government policies, or use the pulpit to mobilise their followers to pressure the government, or push aggressively to gain ground at the expense of other groups, this must lead to trouble."

    Significantly, Wong included secular groups in the equation ("Every group, whether religious or secular, has to live and let live, to exercise restraint and show mutual respect and tolerance. If any group pushes its agenda aggressively, there will be strong reactions from the other groups."), indicating that they too have a claim for space in the "spaces" set-up.

10. Information from personal interviews with Archbishop John Chew (5 Aug. 2009) and Josie Lau (10 Aug. 2009).

References

Channel News Asia, 30 July 2002, "SDP Chief fined for violating Public Entertainments Exemption Order".

Lee Hsien Loong, 2009, National Day Rally Speech at the University Cultural Centre, National University of Singapore, 16 August, <http://www.pmo.gov. sg/News/Messages/National+Day+Rally+Speech+2009+Part+3+Racial+and +Religious+Harmony.htm> [accessed 12 Oct. 2009].

The Online Citizen, 24 April 2009, "Staff sent out email asking members to vote at AWARE EOGM", by Terence Lee and Deborah Choo, <http://theonlinecitizen. com/2009/04/breaking-news-staff-sent-out-emails-asking-members-to-vote-at-aware-eogm/> [accessed 17 Oct. 2009].

The Straits Times, 3 Feb. 2002, "S'pore at risk if races assert separate identities", by Susan Long.

_____, 9 Feb. 2002, "Common uniform policy strengthens national unity", by Ahmad Osman and G. Sivakkumaran.

_____, 26 May 2002, "DPM Lee slams ex-Fateha chief for PAS visits".

_____, 13 Sept. 2002, "Malaysian lawyer won't get to fight tudung case".

_____, 20 April 2009, "Dangerous turn in domestic dispute", by Paul Jacob.

_____, 24 April 2009a, "Dr Thio upset about sexuality programme", by Zakir Hussain.

_____, 24 April 2009b, "Lawyer's key role in AWARE coup", by Zakir Hussain.

_____, 25 April 2009, "Old guard members counter allegations of pro-gay stance", by Wong Kim Hoh.

_____, 29 April 2009, "MOE: No complaints from parents, Dr Thio", Forum Page, by Sum Chee Wah, Director, Education Programmes, Ministry of Education.

_____, 30 April 2009, "AWARE moves to Suntec after police veto Expo venue", by Wong Kim Hoh.

_____, 1 May 2009a, "MOE now looking into sexuality programme", by Theresa Tan and Amelia Tan.

_____, 1 May 2009b, "Churches should stay out of AWARE Tussle", by Zakir Hussain and Wong Kim Hoh.

_____, 7 May 2009, "Why MOE suspended AWARE project", Forum Page, by Jennifer Chan, Press Secretary to Minister for Education.

_____, 18 May 2009, "Gay activists a key constituency of AWARE", Forum Page, by Thio Su Mien.

_____, 22 May 2009, "AWARE rivalry slammed", by Theresa Tan and Amelia Tan.

_____, 10 Sept. 2009, "Advice to main media: Stay balanced", by Clarissa Oon.

Thio, Li-ann, 2009, Singapore Parliament Hansard, Parliament No. 11, Session 2, Vol. 86, Sitting No. 3, 26 May 2009, Presidents Address, <http://www. parliament.gov.sg:80/reports/public/hansard/title/2009.0526/20090526_S0005_ T0001.ftml#1> [accessed 17 Oct. 2009].

White Paper on the Maintenance of Religious Harmony, 1989. Singapore: Singapore National Printers.

Wong Kan Seng, 2009, Press Release from the Ministry of Home Affairs, 15 May, <http://www.mha.gov.sg/news_details.aspx?nid=MTQ0MA%3d%3d-H1alkdl4Ksw%3d> [accessed 17 Oct. 2009].

CHAPTER 4

Who Dragged Christianity into the AWARE Saga?: Observations on the Role of Christians, Value Pluralism and Contestation in Public Discourse

Eugene K.B. Tan

Introduction

With 85 per cent of Singaporeans professing to belong to a religion, religion forms a core part of many Singaporeans' identities and value systems. That religion and politics are not distinct and mutually exclusive spheres of influence and experience is also recognised by the state.[1] The Association of Women for Action and Research (AWARE) dispute started quite innocuously, with initial indications being that of an internal spat that occurs once in a while in the nascent civil society space.[2] As it is well-known by now, a group of relatively new and unknown members (the "new guard") assumed control of AWARE at its annual general meeting in March 2009. The long-established stalwarts (the "old guard") complacently failed to see the signs when applications for new memberships spiked in the lead up to the annual general meeting. But this was no ordinary leadership change or renewal. The installation of the new leadership in AWARE set in motion a series of events, culminating in the hot-tempered extraordinary general meeting (EGM), called by the old guard, in May 2009.

The dispute quickly transmogrified into an apparent existential contest for survival amidst the drama of accusations and mud-slinging, death threats, and concerted actions by the two protagonist camps to get as many supporters as possible signed up as members who would attend the EGM. The stakes were seemingly high. Whoever had control of AWARE was potentially well-placed to set the agenda, influence the direction and focus of feminism and gender equality work in Singapore. What exactly was the AWARE saga all about? Was it just another internal dispute between members over the direction of one of Singapore's most well-known women's organisation? Or was it a more fundamental fight over the soul of AWARE? Was the AWARE dispute a proxy battle over the normative character of the Singaporean nation? Was religion and/or homosexuality a central issue in the dispute or mere smokescreens? Or was religion a straw man and homosexuality a scapegoat? If religion had nothing to do with the dispute, who "dragged" religion into it?

This chapter seeks to examine the role Christianity was perceived to have played in the AWARE dispute. It examines the various perspectives from various groups of Christians, and the state.[3] The essay is not about the Anglican Church of Our Saviour (COOS) where key members of the new AWARE Exco worshipped, although the discussion will outline some features of evangelical Christianity. Neither does this essay set out to determine if the AWARE dispute was about conservative Christianity overreaching in the secular realm. It is outside the scope of this essay to determine the state of mind of the protagonists.

Rather, this chapter has a more modest objective. It seeks, primarily, to examine how Christianity featured in the dispute and the responses it elicited from various stakeholders. Although the COOS featured prominently in the AWARE saga, the dispute did not just concern and impacted the COOS. The larger Christian community was vicariously involved and concerned. Indeed, while the dispute ostensibly involved and implicated Christians, it also raised significant questions about the role of religion in the public square. The dispute, the protagonists and the stakeholders did not operate within a vacuum. Their actions, their thoughts and their beliefs were motivated by their perceptions, understanding and concerns with societal developments.

The other part of the chapter examines two overarching issues that the AWARE dispute raised. The first relates to the growing value pluralism and the contestation of values in Singapore society. The second issue is on the place of religion in the public sphere. A consequence of value pluralism is the greater likelihood of deep conflict over social and moral norms in Singapore society. I argue that given the co-existence of different normative positions on deeply contested issues, a live-and-let-live attitude is necessary since an all-or-nothing approach would strain social cohesion and stress the social fabric unnecessarily. Diversity and difference are foundational cornerstones for pluralism in a society. In tandem with increased piety in Singapore society, civil society is already experiencing the increased profile of religious groups, religious views and religious identities in the public sphere. Religious groups are part and parcel of civil society. I argue that this interface of the private and the public is not only an enterprise that is heavily value-laden but that it will heighten the contestation of values. Thus, it is imperative for Singapore society to manage such contestation if such contestation is not to result in confrontation and the destruction of value pluralism.

* * *

At AWARE's annual general meeting on 28 March 2009, elections for its office-bearers produced nine (out of 12) new faces in the executive committee (Exco).[4] The new Exco members had apparently joined AWARE within the previous 12 months. *The Straits Times* first brought this "changing of the guard" at AWARE to the public attention (*The Straits Times* 10 April 2009). The subsequent drama that rapidly unfolded in the short but intense few weeks between end March and early May 2009 attracted a lot of media attention, especially within the English-language print media, and in new media as well.

Taking prime position in the media spotlight was the news that six members of AWARE's new guard Exco and their "feminist mentor", well-known senior lawyer Dr Thio Su Mien, attended the Anglican Church of Our Saviour (COOS) at Margaret Drive. COOS has a strong stance against the promotion of homosexuality as a normal lifestyle although it emphasises that it is not homophobic or anti-homosexual (Hong 2009).[5] In particular, it is stridently against gay-affirming movements and programmes that seek to advance homosexuality as normal.

The new guard's Exco indicated that it was their deep concern of AWARE's Comprehensive Sex Education (CSE) programme for teenagers in national schools that motivated their seeking office in AWARE. They felt that the CSE programme's philosophy and instruction was ambivalent, if not friendly, towards homosexuality. Consequently, this raised the question what constituted "normal" sexuality and whether school-children in AWARE's CSE programme were imbibing inappropriate values. In the lead-up to the EGM, the new guard made strenuous efforts to clarify that their position on homosexuality was one of "love the sinner but not the sin". They thus sought to distinguish homosexuals from homosexual acts. The new guard's efforts to entrench heterosexual universality and preference for pro-family values naturally gave rise to the related characterisation that the dispute pitted Christianity and homosexuality.

By now the stage was set for a bruising battle in the EGM, both in support and against the actions of the new guard Exco. It was therefore not at all surprising that, intended or not, the AWARE dispute was already actively mobilising Christians and the homosexual community.

"Responsible" Interventions by Christian Elites and the Authorities

On Sunday, 26 April 2009, COOS Senior Pastor Derek Hong brought the raging dispute to a boil. In a sermon at the COOS, he urged the women in his congregation to "be engaged" in the AWARE dispute by supporting the new guard Exco president Josie Lau (a member of COOS) and her "sisters" in the Exco at AWARE's EGM. In particular, Senior Pastor Hong's well-reported remarks (and well-repeated in cyberspace) that generated a lot of ire were: "It's not a crusade against the people but there's a line that God has drawn for us, and we don't want our nation crossing the line." This reference to a "crusade" and the nation not to cross "the line" evoked and insinuated the moral depravity of new guard Exco's "adversaries". Not surprisingly, the sermon was interpreted as a call to action for Christian women who were AWARE members to be at the EGM and to cast votes in support of the new guard Exco.[6] The tenor of Senior Pastor Ong's remarks alluded to a doomsday scenario if Christians did not make their stand clear in the AWARE dispute. In that Sunday church service, the pastor had also invited the congregation to pray for Lau and her husband.

On 30 April 2009, two days before the "showdown" EGM, the National Council of Churches of Singapore (NCCS)[7] made a "timely" intervention. It issued a public statement signed by Archbishop Dr John Chew, then NCCS President, and General Secretary of NCCS Lim K. Tham, which is reproduced below in full:

> The National Council of Churches has been following the recent events related to AWARE. We are concerned that religion has been dragged into the unfortunate situation. The matters related to AWARE

should be solved by its own members. We do not condone churches getting involved in this matter; neither do we condone pulpits being used for this purpose. Our member churches are not involved in the present saga. In fact, our heads of churches have very recently reiterated to their clergy the standing instruction on the proper use of the pulpit.

This does not preclude individual Christians, like all their fellow-citizens, from contributing in matters of social concern and well-being. Nor does it preclude churches from being involved in public square discussions within the rules of engagement in a multi-religious society that Singapore is. On various occasions in the past, the NCCS has done so responsibly when called upon to give our opinions or when there was a need to add our voice. We believe that we can engage together in our common spaces in a spirit of mutual respect so that we can contribute positively to the well-being of our nation.

In this particular situation, we should all step back and give AWARE space to settle its own matters.[8]

Of significance was NCCS's view that "religion has been dragged into the unfortunate situation" and that "Our member churches are not involved in the present saga." In essence, the statement clarified that Christian congregations under the NCCS umbrella ought not to be mobilised for the purposes of the EGM. The NCCS's statement, however, did not say anything new with regards to the norms of religious conduct by church leaders and the congregations. Nonetheless, the importance and timeliness of the statement cannot be over-emphasised, notwithstanding that the NCCS was urged by the Internal Security Department to make a public statement.[9] In urging Christians to "step back", it signaled that the AWARE dispute, in particular the EGM, was not an occasion for the churches and their congregations to be engaged in directly. In the larger scheme of things, the EGM was not a spiritual "call to arms" or a spiritual crusade that engaged Christians had to take in order to protect their faith.

If the intent of the NCCS's public statement of 30 April 2009 was not clear enough, it would be made so the following day — the eve of AWARE's EGM. COOS Senior Pastor Derek Hong issued a statement in which he agreed with Archbishop John Chew that "the pulpit should not have been used in this AWARE saga". Hong expressed regret that his actions "on the pulpit have aroused some tension in this saga. I now stand corrected. I undertake to be more sensitive to similar situations in the future."

These statements, by NCCS and Senior Pastor Hong, suggest that by the eve of the EGM, any remaining doubt that religion did not feature in the AWARE dispute was laid to rest. Even if religion was not part of the original equation, it was now immaterial whether Christianity was dragged in or not into AWARE's dispute. Christianity was in the spotlight. The developments in the lead-up to the EGM made it abundantly clear that religion was an involved player by choice or by default.

The induced interventions of NCCS and Senior Pastor Hong operated as timely counsel and an important signal to the faith-inspired stakeholders in the dispute that the AWARE dispute was not a spiritual war. The NCCS's characterisation that "religion has been dragged into the unfortunate situation" deliberately left unclear who dragged religion into the dispute.

Earlier, on 29 April 2009, the police advised Singapore Expo, a convention venue, not to allow AWARE's application to hold its EGM there. The police were concerned "of the strong possibility that a coming together of members and supporters of the opposing camps at the same venue may result in law and order problems" (*The Straits Times* 30 April 2009). Although the police did not mention the linkage, a two-day Christian conference, "Transformation 2009", was scheduled to be held at the Singapore Expo on 1 and 2 May. According to the same *Straits Times* report, there were concerns that "people attending the conference would swamp the AWARE meeting and outnumber supporters of the old guard hugely".[10] AWARE subsequently held its EGM at Suntec City. While one could say that the recommendation by the police was a precautionary measure, it also suggested that the police had assessed that the AWARE dispute was already stoking emotions to a frenzy. As such, the EGM potentially posed serious public order and security concerns given the conscious efforts on the part of both camps to mobilise as many supporters to attend the EGM.

The Catholic Church's Perspective[11]

To all intents and purposes, Christianity was "involved" in the AWARE dispute. Although the COOS was a key protagonist, the dispute was of abiding interest to the other Protestant churches and the Catholic Church. The brewing dispute was already generating concerns over the extent of religious encroachment into secular civil society space, and this exercised the various Christian denominations. Christians were sufficiently moved to ask themselves and of their churches what was the right stand to take. The need for pastoral guidance was palpable in light of the perceptions that faith-inspired values were at stake and under attack in the dispute.

Catholic Archbishop Nicholas Chia was sufficiently moved to clarify the Catholic Church's stance on the role of religion in the secular realm. Archbishop Chia said "Secular organisations like AWARE should remain secular. These organisations are secular and are not within our ambit." The Archbishop added that "Religious organisations can give their points of view, but we don't go into (the secular organisation's) affairs." The Archbishop also directed Catholic priests in the archdiocese not to comment on the AWARE matter (*The Straits Times* 3 May 2009).

Subsequently, after the EGM, the Caritas Singapore Community Council (CSCC) elaborated that the Archbishop's remarks did not contradict the Church's social mission.[12] The CSCC published an article in *The Catholic News*, the official newspaper of the Catholic Church in Singapore, wherein it stated that the Church's role "is not to canvass the support of Catholics for a particular political party or civil society faction. Its role is to teach Catholics what is true and morally right, and inform their consciences so they are able to make good political choices." The article acknowledged that a Catholic's perspective and views on the AWARE dispute may be shaped by the teachings of the Catholic Church:

> There is a dangerous and mistaken belief among some that citizens taking part in secular affairs should leave their religiously-informed views behind. As citizens, Catholics and those of other religions have every right to take part in civil society. They can form associations or join existing ones with the aim of putting across their point of view, but how they choose to do so matters a great deal.

It further opined that Christians in pursuing their faith-inspired convictions and values in the public sphere "must not employ unethical means to achieve their ends, no matter how noble". The article observed that the process and method employed by the new guard Exco may lack legitimacy in the eyes of the general public:

> The AWARE saga was an example of Christians trying to bring about change through means that many found questionable and unacceptable. They may have gone in with the best intentions in the world. They may have had an admirable goal — to end what they saw as AWARE's promotion of a gay and lesbian lifestyle. But in the end, they appeared to have lost both moral authority and credibility because

of the means they are perceived to have used to capture control of AWARE. Their actions ultimately provoked a backlash which led to their ouster within two months of being elected the group's leaders.

The article provided assurance that there was nothing wrong even if one's convictions in a secular world were driven by faith. Consistent with the Church's Principle of Participation,[13] individuals, whether Catholic or not, have a right and duty to participate in the AWARE dispute, in accordance with their convictions. However, it advised that, "We should communicate our views in terms that others in a secular society can understand. We should not scheme to defeat those who hold contrary views, or use coercion of any kind to sway others, for surely, we too would object strenuously if those of other faiths were to try to impose their religious beliefs on us."

In the Aftermath of the EGM — the Government Has Its Say

With the conclusion of the EGM, a "ceasefire" of sorts ensued. It was now opportune for the government to "step in", mediate and offer its views and counsel. About two weeks after the EGM on 14 May 2009, Deputy Prime Minister and then Home Affairs Minister Wong Kan Seng made the government's first substantive observations on the AWARE dispute. Wong's remarks were carefully calibrated and addressed to the different stakeholders in the AWARE dispute. They were widely reported in the local media the following day, and provide insights into the government's perspective of the dispute.

At the outset, DPM Wong reiterated the government's position on homosexuality and stressed that it was not going to change regardless of which group helmed AWARE. DPM Wong stated that Singapore society was "basically a conservative society and the conventional family, a heterosexual stable family, is the norm and the building block of our society", while also adding that "homosexuals are part of our society ... and are entitled to their private lives" (Wong 2009). He also reminded the homosexual community to "accept the informal limits which reflect the point of balance that our society can accept, and not to assert themselves stridently as gay groups do in the West". Without elaborating on what these "informal limits" were, DPM Wong advised gay groups not to assert themselves too stridently. This suggested that the government's own assessment was that the gay groups were also actively involved in the AWARE saga.

DPM Wong referred to the public perception that the new guard protagonists were motivated by their faith, and the way the so-called battle lines were drawn pointed to an ostensible cultural war involving homosexuals and a group of Christians. According to DPM Wong,

> [The government] was worried about the disquieting public percep-
> tion that a group of conservative Christians, all attending the same
> church, which held strong views on homosexuality, had moved in
> and taken over AWARE because they disapproved of what AWARE
> had been doing. This raised many qualms among non-Christians, and
> also among Christians who believed that this was an unwise move in
> a multi-racial, multi-religious society. It was much more dangerous
> because now religion was also getting involved, and it was no longer
> just the issue of homosexuality.

The central role of the religious elites in guiding their congregations was again underlined. DPM Wong spoke approvingly of the "clear
statement" of 30 April 2009 by the NCCS that it did not condone
churches getting involved in the AWARE dispute. He welcomed the
fact that leaders of different religious faiths had also come out to
reinforce the NCCS message: "Their statements provided clear guidance
to their followers.... Had it not been for these sober statements from
religious leaders, we would have had serious problems." This was a
further acknowledgement that the government viewed the then rapidly
evolving developments at AWARE as one which pitted religion and
homosexuality.

DPM Wong also took the opportunity to spell out three key "rules
of engagement". The first was that "[r]eligious individuals have the
same rights as any citizen to express their views on issues in the public
space, as guided by their teachings and personal conscience. However,
like every citizen, they should always be mindful of the sensitivities of
living in a multi-religious society.... This calls for tolerance, accom-
modation, and give and take on all sides." Secondly, DPM Wong reiterated the need to keep religion and politics separate. "If religious
groups start to campaign to change certain government policies, or
use the pulpit to mobilise their followers to pressure the government,
or push aggressively to gain ground at the expense of other groups,
this must lead to trouble." Thirdly, the political arena must always be
secular. DPM Wong noted that even as religious groups and individuals
"set the moral tone of our society, and are a source of strength in
times of adversity", "our laws and policies do not derive from religious

authority, but reflect the judgments and decisions of the secular Government and Parliament to serve the national interest and collective good". He rationalised that in applying the laws and public policies equally, the system generated confidence if it provided "equal treatment and protection for all, regardless of which group one happens to belong to".

On the same day, through its then Vice-President (Methodist) Bishop Dr Robert Solomon, the NCCS responded to DPM Wong's remarks. It expressed its support for the government's stand. The NCCS also took the opportunity to reiterate that:

> The majority of Singaporeans, including Christians and people of other faiths, hold to the traditional heterosexual family values that the government has promised to preserve in our society. This is important if we want to maintain harmony and confidence in our society. The government has also stated that lobbying against this position is not going to change its policy. I think the message calls for people to accept this position and not push lifestyles or values that will only cause strong reactions and disrupt the harmony in our society. (National Council of Churches of Singapore 14 May 2009)

In this second statement, the NCCS reiterated its earlier stance that "religion was unnecessarily dragged into the debate" and that while churches should not get involved in the internal matters of a secular organisation like AWARE, this "did not preclude individual Christians and churches from engaging in public square issues within the rules of engagement".

The NCCS also felt that Christians had been unfairly spotlighted in the AWARE dispute. It stated that "the majority of Singaporeans, regardless of race or religion, have a common conservative view [on the issue of homosexuality]. It would not be helpful to single out Christians in this regard." The NCCS chose to characterise the dispute as "more an issue between the majority of Singaporeans and a minority with different views rather than between the church and others".

This second NCCS statement was both defensive of the role attributed to Christians and yet assertive of the Christian role and perspective *vis-à-vis* homosexuality. At issue was the perceived militant gay agenda which sought to normalise alternative family structures on an equal footing as the traditional family. It indicated that the NCCS felt that Christians were compelled to act because the homosexual community was too blatant in pushing their lifestyles and values, threatening the traditional heterosexual family values that the government had promised to preserve. It was a subtle message to the powers-that-be that they must preserve the equilibrium if religious groups were not to seek self-help in order to maintain the moral tone of Singapore society.

Between the EGM and the National Day Rally on 16 August 2009, many government Ministers made oblique references to the AWARE saga when they made appeals to Singaporeans to be mindful of the need to maintain inter-religious harmony. Prime Minister Lee Hsien Loong used the prominent platform of the annual National Day Rally (NDR) to make his first remarks on the AWARE dispute. Prefacing his remarks on the AWARE dispute, PM Lee described the backdrop of race and religion as "the most visceral and dangerous fault line" in our society. Given DPM Wong's remarks in May that year, PM Lee stated more directly the government's concerns in the AWARE saga:

> But what worried us was that this was an attempt by a religiously motivated group who shared a strong religious fervour to enter civil space, take over an NGO it disapproved of and impose its agenda. And it was bound to provoke a push back from groups who held the opposite view which happened vociferously and stridently as a fierce battle. (Lee 2009)

Like DPM Wong, PM Lee acknowledged the role of religious elites, in particular the leaders of the Christian congregations, in diffusing the tension through their "very responsible stand" in statements to them "because had these statements not been made, we would have had a very serious problem".

The Prime Minister identified three potential risks of religious fervour: aggressive proselytisation, intolerance and disrespect of the religious beliefs of others, and exclusiveness through not interacting with people of other faiths. He pointed out that intolerance could be a source of deep division — not just in our society but also within families. PM Lee went on to reiterate the four basic rules for religious harmony: (1) all groups to exercise tolerance and restraint; (2) keep religion and politics separate; (3) the government must remain secular; and (4) preserve the common space that all Singaporeans share regardless of affiliations.

These ground rules are not new — they are found, for instance, in the Declaration on Religious Harmony. The challenge is to enable these rules to embed the norms and values so that they entrench the shared commitment to religious harmony while also providing for common rules of engagement and conduct. Laws by themselves cannot foster sustainable inter-faith understanding and engagement. Instead, they may provide a false sense of security and stability. PM Lee concluded with a calibrated caution, using a trope familiar to Abrahamaic faiths of Christianity, Islam and Judaism, urging Singaporeans to maintain the "Garden of Eden state" here where Singaporeans "are happy, where things are working…. If you leave the Garden of Eden, you cannot get back in again."

Value Pluralism and Contestation: Where Does the Secular End and the Sacred Begin?

The seeming absence of overt religious conflict in Singapore may have given rise to a false consciousness and complacency that racial and religious harmony is a natural state of affairs here. Religious freedom, guaranteed by Singapore's constitution, has led to the casual comfort that one can say and do what one believes one's faith exhorts, impervious to how it may affect others. But tact, honesty, open minds and a commitment to unity are essential preconditions if differences that impinge upon race, religion and — increasingly — values are not to tear Singaporean society apart. In this regard, the existential threat to Singapore is not increased religious piety and fervour *per se* but *how* that religiosity is exercised.

The Prime Minister's clarion call to the nation alluded to the urgent imperative and need for the management of race and religion to evolve from a "whole-of-government" to a "whole-of-society" approach. Governments alone cannot maintain sustainable peace and harmony. Yet, the so-called strict separation of the secular and religious realms does not hold for people of faith, in particular Christians and Muslims. The Manichean dichotomy of the secular (public) and religious (private) realms is not only artificial, but privileges rationality and public reason. Religion cannot be artificially separated from society since the pursuit of one's private conscience will manifest itself in the public domain through informing a person's perspective on issues that impact upon one's sense of moral self-worth and purpose. In short, one cannot expel religion from the public space.

As the AWARE dispute vividly demonstrated, Christians believe that they have a moral duty to be informed by and to act on their Christian values. The AWARE dispute, nonetheless, drew attention to questions such as how the centrifugal tendencies of value pluralism can enable individuals to live in accordance with their own conceptions of what gives them meaning and value in life within a secular regime that prioritises public order. Similarly, the gay and lesbian community pondered over whether their space in Singapore is at the behest and forbearance of the majority, and whether their status will be accorded formal rights. To be sure, the situation in Singapore is not unique (see Sachs 2009, for the South African situation).

At one level, the AWARE dispute reflects the evolving complexity in Singapore society. While seemingly resolved for now, the issues surrounding the leadership tussle within AWARE point to the evolving diversity and innate complexity in a fast-changing society. The divisive and ugly divide exposed by the dispute reflects the putative battle-ground that Singapore potentially would encounter in the years ahead. As Singapore becomes more diverse and complex as a society, the contestation will invariably shift towards more subtle but inherently substantive forms of differences, especially those inflected by competing and, perhaps contesting, ethical, moral and religious convictions. As the AWARE dispute demonstrated, the dogmatism, fervour and commitment with which some of these beliefs and convictions are pursued will only raise the stakes.

At its core, the chasm in the AWARE dispute pivots on a keen — almost existential — contestation over values. Specifically, the sort of values and causes that AWARE should endorse, promote and be identified with. For instance, the AWARE dispute presented the state's and the majority's ordering of public values. In turn, these values form the basis on which public policies are crafted, laws made, and the hierarchal relationship between competing values. As such, the AWARE dispute affirmed that the conventional family of "a heterosexual stable family" is prioritised, preferred and defended — with alternative life-style and family arrangements that do not conform to it being subordinated. Because of the faith-inspired inflection or inspiration, the dispute became even more complex, more fractious, with seemingly more at stake.

The issues the AWARE dispute highlighted were not solely over the rights of homosexuals. Instead, they pointed more to the deep conflict over social and moral norms in Singapore society, especially when the commitment to the family is *prima facie* abiding, prominent and strong. At the same time, the juxtaposition of seemingly unrelated issues in the AWARE controversy suggests that the necessary and growing diversity of Singapore's society is a potential "battle-ground" in the years ahead. In some respects, the AWARE dispute foreshadowed the landscape of salient fault-lines and putative divides in Singaporean society.

This was evidenced by the *déjà vu* feel to the AWARE saga. This values contestation is not new at all. But what was new was that religion was in the cauldron more prominently, more assertively this time — regardless of whether Christianity was dragged in, co-opted, or mobilised as a rallying cry or justification for the actions. The passionate advocacy, the exuberant debates, the systematic mobilisation of support, and the ugly resort to threats, insults and holier-than-thou attitude were par for the course and were experienced in the recent past. Take for instance, keeping Section 377A of the Penal Code (this provision criminalises homosexual sex between consenting male adults) on the statute books and, to a lesser extent, on removing the ban on casino gaming in Singapore. Indeed, the AWARE dispute can be seen as the continuation of unresolved matters and simmering tension from the divisive debate in 2007 over Section 377A of the Penal Code.

For the new guard Exco, it would appear that wresting control of AWARE would enable it to moderate the apparent excesses and liberal inclinations of AWARE. That in itself would be an important moral victory and facilitate the right-sizing of AWARE to its supposed original purpose. Some Christians also saw society's moral fibre and norms coming under siege through an increasingly morally lax society. On the other hand, the homosexuals — who perceived their lifestyles and value systems to be under attack — mobilised in support of the old guard. This aggressive push-back, according to AWARE former President, Braema Mathi (2009: 15), "may have consolidated gay activism here as the community bands even more strongly around efforts to deny them space". The gay community saw the AWARE dispute as an opportunity to challenge the structural conditions (such as norms, laws, policies, institutions, habits, symbols) that they believe marginalised and stigmatised homosexuals. They rallied to challenge the assertion and belief that the gay community's freedom must be limited (or even extinguished) so that it accords with the supposed moral standards of the community.

Because of the issues at stake and the constituencies affected, the dispute within AWARE naturally drew into the fray various groupings including gay individuals and activist groups, as well as those opposed to homosexuality, parents with school-going children and Christians.

Formally, the old guard Exco prevailed at the EGM and regained control of AWARE. However, the deeper issues remained unresolved. To seek resolution in such a convoluted mix is perhaps unrealistic given the fundamentally different worldviews and starting points held by the protagonists. Yet, the AWARE dispute, arguably, did not produce a reasoned, mature and principled engagement of the issues pertaining to the dispute. Nonetheless, contestation is necessary and a prelude to engagement, understanding, and agreeing to disagree. Often, it is through contestation that an airing of contrasting value positions are better understood. And this may result in a compromise, if not resolution. At the very least, even if there is no resolution to the differences, the different actors would be exposed to contrasting perspectives, value systems and propositions. In the final analysis, the AWARE dispute generated a lot of talk and noise but little dialogue. Moral panic was also liberally resorted to by both camps.

Going forward, putative conflicts and disagreements in Singapore are likely to be normative, centering on differences in values, morals and norms, as informed by different ethical systems of which religion is a key value-system. To be clear, religion and increased piety are not a problem in and of itself. But the larger concern in the AWARE dispute resided for both camps in a moral logic that was seemingly undergirded by uncompromising values.

Yet it is worth noting that moral standing or legitimacy is not a zero-sum game in which the granting of a concession or to adopt a "live-and-let-live" attitude is akin to an abject moral failure. Ultimately, in a multi-racial and multi-religious society and for civil society to thrive, dignity, recognition and respect are needed at a most fundamental level. Such an attitude applies equally to minority groups that exist outside the mainstream.

Can and should Singaporeans expect unanimity on controversial normative issues? No, since unanimity is, in all probability, pitching at too high an expectation. Given the diversity and complexity of Singapore, unanimity on ethically controversial is at odds with the pluralist nature of Singapore society. Does this then mean that a *laissez-faire* attitude and approach is the way to go? Or, is the other extreme of value monism preferred? No, in both instances that would mean the possibility of too many fractures, disagreements and dissidence. This would be detrimental for social cohesiveness. For a multi-racial, multi-religious and multi-lingual society to maintain order, coherence and resilience, the need to arrive at a consensus on fundamental normative issues is crucial. One such area of consensus would be the acceptance of diversity of different positions.

In short, where agreement cannot be arrived at, the disputants should accept the co-existence of different normative positions on relevant issues. This live-and-let-live attitude embodies the sincere recognition that an all-or-nothing approach would be bruising to social cohesion and strain the social fabric unnecessarily. It also recognises that there is room for diversity under the Singapore sun, and that diversity and difference are foundational cornerstones for pluralism in a society.

Religion and Civil Society

In the AWARE dispute, one group of Christians was apparently rising to the challenges of a Singaporean society that was seen to be increasingly liberal in social mores and lax in moral tone. For many Christians, this nihilistic or godless social context is epitomised in the perceived social acceptability of gay and lesbian chic, the apparent official nonchalance towards homosexuality in the face of quest for the "pink dollars", Singapore's aspiration to a global "happening" city, as well as the perceived increasing popularity and acceptability of homosexuality, especially among the younger people, in Singapore (see Heng 2001; Tan 2009). For these Christians, there has to be a moral backlash or blowback as a result of the moral laxity in society. For them, the declining morality in the public domain necessitated a resurgence of public morality (see Thio 2009).

One dominant characterisation of the AWARE saga was that it was about religion, specifically Christianity of the conservative and evangelical strand, either creeping (voluntary) into or being dragged (involuntary) into secular space. In this characterisation, the discourse was one of missionary zeal, perhaps even exuberant religious over-reaching, which galvanised the new guard protagonists into action *vis-à-vis* AWARE. Specifically, their actions were grounded in fundamentalist Christian religious values. They sought to influence and mould Singapore society through those Christian values and teachings, persuaded that it was for the greater good. This charge of being motivated by religious impulses is, of course, strenuously denied by them. Instead, they have stood by their contention that the dispute had everything to do with wholesome family values, feminism, and the vibrancy and health of AWARE as the leading women's organisation in Singapore. That it was secular motivations that resonated with the majority of Singaporeans, which underlined their actions.

This brings us to the place of religious groups, religious views and religious identities in the public sphere. Lest it be forgotten, religious groups are an integral part of civil society. A normative function of civil society is the discretionary shaping of the home/host society. For religious groups, this normative function makes it unlikely that such groups will diverge too greatly from their faith-driven vision of and aspirations for what society should be like. Shaping the future of a society, whether by religious or secular groups, is an enterprise that is heavily value-laden. Here, the contestation of values will assert itself and unless society has a process and a mechanism to manage the contestation, such a contestation will almost surely lead to confrontation and overt conflict.[14]

That aside, Singapore would be all the poorer if secular organisations become fair game for advocacy and activism that are primarily motivated by faith-based beliefs and convictions. There was the palpable concern over allegations of religion mixing with secular matters, accompanied by an aggressive and insensitive proselytisation (Hamilton-Hart 2009). While it is arguable whether a religious group indeed sought to take over AWARE, a secular organisation, it cannot be denied that a driving motivation behind key individuals in the new guard Exco was heavily accented with values and morals derived from a common religious background (see Goh 2010).

Further, the attempt to rally the COOS congregation to get involved in the AWARE EGM as a religious duty was also perceived to be one in which a religious group was making its presence and its ethos felt outside the confines of their church. There is nothing wrong with faith-based values activism and advocacy but the platforms for that sort of advocacy ought to remain within faith groups in the religious sphere, or in groups where the faith-based agenda is clearly spelt out. That way, the intentions, agenda and motivations are clear and better understood.[15]

In the larger effort to develop the common and shared space, Singaporeans need to be alive to the dark side of civil society. Civil society can be uncivil. In Singapore's context, the dark side of civil society is its potential to undermine or destroy the foundational ethos of society such as multi-racialism and meritocracy, as well as degrading the quality of democracy and participation. In short, bad social capital is generated from such uncivil societies. "Bad" civil society impoverishes and destroys social capital, understood here as relationships of trust and reciprocity. Given the emphasis on a harmonious society in Singapore, open contestation and confrontation are frowned upon.

Nonetheless, in the AWARE saga, the brash in-your-face type of advocacy and activism, publicity-seeking histrionics and inducing moral panic were all par for the course. Both sides demonised each other, painting outlandish scenarios that would pan out if the other side won. As Habermas (2010a) questioned recently: "Does participation in democratic procedures have only the functional meaning of silencing a defeated minority, or does it have the deliberative meaning of including the arguments of citizens in the democratic process of opinion- and will-formation?"

To be fair, the AWARE dispute inspired collective activism and ignited exuberant advocacy, and, at times, strident and vociferous debate and confrontational mobilisation of support. Such passionate displays of civic advocacy and imagination have been far and few in Singapore. Faith-inspired groups add another dimension, even if often transcendental in outlook and aspiration, to the possibilities, problems and provocations thrown up by the determined advocacy, vigorous activism and passionate debates. Indeed, it is precisely civic engagement and experience, encompassing the broad spectrum of associational activity and involvement that can help in the development of a country's shared community space and the people's sense of belonging. So there is much to commend in the AWARE dispute.

Much as civil society is in essence a process of democratic deliberation, the mutual exchange of ideas, views and critiques has tremendous potential in scaling up civic discourse and participation by citizens in areas they deem important. Such a process should result in the paradoxical outcome of better governance but with less government. After all, governments do not have a monopoly of wisdom and know-how. The bottom line is that civil society actors must eschew thinking and operating in narrow, self-interested ways inflected by a sense of moral superiority. In disagreements over values, disputants should not insist that any concession, where given, is an admission of the giver's inferior moral standing.

By the same token, civil society actors must strenuously avoid demonising their "opponents". Such a rigid moral logic only undermines the centrality of civil society as an associational space of tolerance, autonomy, respect and dignity. Instead, social learning is a necessary value. Social learning includes the socially constitutive processes of persuasion, cooperation and socialisation, which can provide an institutional hedge against mistrust between and within communities, and between the faith communities and the government. They attempt to regulate conduct and promote the strategic and normative goal of entrenching healthy and respectful value pluralism as a *sine qua non* in a plural society where consensus-seeking is desired and promoted. Respect and recognition for others who do not share the same set of ideals are absolutely vital if Singaporeans are not to allow the differences to become divisive.[16]

The AWARE dispute patently demonstrated that, as a society, Singaporeans urgently need to learn how to avoid abrasive and divisive conflicts over diversity. Where Singaporeans cannot resolve them, they will need to manage differences when disagreements and disputes do occur. This is especially so when the basis of a conflict and disagreement is intractable, with starting points so irreconcilable, that a decisive resolution cannot be expected.

In Lieu of a Conclusion

In accordance with the fundamental liberty of religious freedom under Singapore's Constitution, Singaporeans are entitled to profess, practise and propagate their religious beliefs and seek to create a societal setting that is conducive for the expression and propagation of those beliefs and values. The Constitution also provides for equality below the law and equal protection of the law. But constitutional mandates and niceties aside, the key question is how Singaporeans go about achieving those constitutional goals, not whether they can express and propagate those beliefs and values. Given that Singapore society is becoming more diverse, it is imperative to emphasise a cooperative value-based culture and norms to meet the objectives of ethical conduct grounded in self-regulation, civic responsibility and social resilience. Where faith matters arise in civil society, Singaporeans should observe the belief-action distinction. Singaporeans are entitled to their beliefs and values, and to propagate them so long as they do not offend the law and the foundational principles that undergird Singapore society.

The acrimonious AWARE dispute showed the best and worst of the fledgling civil society in Singapore. The dispute emphatically demonstrated that Singaporeans do care and can be counted on to protect and promote passionately the values and causes that they believe in.

However, it also demonstrated quite unequivocally that Singapore's civil society still has a long way to go in terms of engaging in a vigorous, yet meaningful, debate. In some respects, the AWARE controversy is a blessing in disguise. It brought to the fore issues that have been simmering in some quarters and provided an opportunity for those concerns to be vented. Hopefully, future disputes can be better managed.

Religion will continue to be a source of succour and spiritual ballast for many Singaporeans in a rapidly changing world. It is an essential part of the individual and collective identities of many Singaporeans. The AWARE dispute vividly demonstrated how religion can provide the ballast for social solidarity and the impetus for political mobilisation. And because religion provides a moral code and a moral framework in everyday life, it has the intrinsic power to mobilise, motivate and enforce behaviour, norms and values. The perennial challenge is to ensure that faith and secular communities continue to recognise and respect the virtues and imperatives of diversity, respect and tolerance. Religion remains highly relevant even in a society where rationality and reason are celebrated, and so does the challenge to properly situate the role of religion and secular reason in public life in Singapore.

Notes

1. See, for example, White Paper on the Maintenance of Religious Harmony (Cmd 21 of 1989).

2. In essence, civil society is the voluntary associational life that lies between the family and institutions of the state. The metaphorical space that civil society occupies is one that is voluntary and plural in nature. It represents the citizens' associational freedom *vis-à-vis* the state. Conventionally, civil society is conceptualised in relation to the state — it is apart from the state but not necessarily on antagonistic terms with the state.

3. I group the various Christian groups collectively as "Christians", using their common faith to identify them generically. This may not be entirely satisfactory since not all Christians shared the same views and supported the actions of the "new guard". Notwithstanding this obvious overgeneralisation, "Christians" is used as a generic term in recognition that this group was either driven to action in the AWARE saga largely because of their Christian faith, or responded to the developments in the AWARE saga informed by their Christian values and teachings.

4. The legality of the elections at the AGM was never challenged.

5. See further COOS website at <http://www.coos.org.sg/index.html>.

6. In his 2 May 2009 sermon to youths at COOS, Senior Pastor Derek Hong described the quest for normal sexuality as a "struggle between light and darkness".

7. The membership of the National Council of Churches of Singapore includes the Anglican Diocese of Singapore, Assemblies of God of Singapore, Lutheran Church in Singapore, Methodist Church in Singapore, Presbyterian Church in Singapore, The Salvation Army, Mar Thomas Syrian Church, St. Thomas Orthodox Syrian Cathedral, Church of Singapore, Evangelical Free Church, and many other independent churches and Christian organisations.

8. Public Statement on AWARE by the National Council of Churches of Singapore, 30 April 2009; available at <http://www.nccs.org.sg/NCCS/Statement_Aware.html>.

9. For details of this development, see chapter by Azhar Ghani and Gillian Koh in this volume.

10. According to the same report, "The Christian conference is being organised by LoveSingapore, an inter-church organisation founded by Pastor Lawrence Khong from the Faith Community Baptist Church. Its committee members are pastors from different churches, including Pastor Derek Hong from the Church of Our Saviour in Margaret Drive, where several of AWARE's leaders worship."

11. The quotes in this section are taken from the article "AWARE and the Principle of Participation", *The Catholic News* (Singapore), 24 May 2009, p. 17. This article was contributed by the Caritas Singapore Community Council (CSCC).

12. The CSCC is the official social and community arm of the Catholic Archdiocese in Singapore.

13. The Principle of Participation exhorts Catholics to have a pro-active role in shaping their present and future lives as well as society as a whole.

14. US President Barack Obama, speaking of the American context with regards to the search for common ground in the divisive and, at times, violent abortion debate, said:

> How does each of us remain firm in our principles, and fight for what we consider right, without demonizing those with just as strongly held convictions on the other side? … the fact is that at some level, the views of the two camps [pro-life and pro-choice] are irreconcilable. Each side will continue to make its case to the public with passion and conviction. But surely we can do so without reducing those with differing views to caricature.

    See his speech at the Notre Dame commencement, 2009. This exhortation is particularly apposite in Singapore's context.

15. By parity of reasoning, it would be highly problematic if a secular group some how manages to take over a group constituted by people who are faith-driven.

16. Jurgen Habermas (2010b) argues that for a constructive dialogue, in an age of religious and ideological fundamentalism, two conditions must be met. The first is that religion must accept the authority of secular reason "as the fallible results of the sciences and the universalistic egalitarianism in law and morality". The second condition is that "secular reason must not position itself as the judge concerning the truths of faith".

References

Goh, Daniel P.S., 2010, "State and Social Christianity in Postcolonial Singapore", *Sojourn: Journal of Social Issues in Southeast Asia* 25, 1: 54–89.

Hamilton-Hart, Natasha, 2009, "Religion, Extremism, and Terrorism: Is There a Link?", Revised paper presented at the 23rd Asia Pacific Roundtable, Kuala Lumpur, 2–4 June.

Harbemas, Jurgen, 2010a, "Leadership and *Leitkultur*", *New York Times*, 26 October.

———, 2010b, *An Awareness of What is Missing*. Oxford: Polity Press.

Heng, Russell Hiang Khng, 2001, "Tiptoe Out of the Closet: The Before and After of the Increasingly Visible Gay Community in Singapore", in *Gay and Lesbian Asia: Culture, Identity and* Community, ed. Gerard Sullivan and Peter A. Jackson. New York: Harrington Park Press.

Hong, Derek, 26 April 2009, "Our Position on Homosexuality", <http://www.coos.org.sg/sermons_sr.php> [accessed 10 Oct. 2009].

Lee Hsien Loong, 16 Aug. 2009, Prime Minister's National Day Rally Speech at the University Cultural Centre, National University of Singapore, <http://www.pmo.gov.sg/News/Messages/National+Day+Rally+Speech+2009+Part+3+Racial+and+Religious+Harmony.htm> [accessed 12 Oct. 2009].

Mathi, Braema, 2009, "Second Wind", *SALT* (July–August): 12–15.

National Council of Churches of Singapore, 30 April 2009, "Aware", <http://www.nccs.org.sg/NCCS/Statement_aware.html> [accessed 10 Oct. 2009].

National Council of Churches of Singapore, 14 May 2009, "Reply to Media Inquiry on DPM's Statement", <http://www.nccs.org.sg/NCCS/Statement_Reply_To_Media_Query_On_DPMs_Statement.html> [accessed 10 Oct. 2009].

Sachs, Albie, 2009, *The Strange Alchemy of Life and Law*. Oxford: Oxford University Press.

Tan, Chris K.K., 2009, "'But They are Like You and Me': Gay Civil Servants and Citizenship in a Cosmopolitanizing Singapore", *City and Society* 21, 1: 133–54.

The Straits Times, 10 April 2009, "Unknowns knock out veterans at AWARE polls", by Wong Kim Hoh.

———, 30 April 2009, "AWARE moves to Suntec after police veto Expo venue", by Wong Kim Hoh.

_____, 2 May 2009. "No direct dealings".

Thio, Li-ann, 2009, *Mind the Gap: Contending for Righteousness in an Age of Lawlessness*. Singapore: Genesis Books.

White Paper on the Maintenance of Religious Harmony, 1989. Singapore: Singapore National Printers.

Wong Kan Seng, 15 May 2009, Press Release from the Ministry of Home Affairs, <http://www.mha.gov.sg/news_details.aspx?nid=MTQ0MA%3D%3D-H1aIkdI4Ksw%3D> [accessed 17 Oct. 2009].

CHAPTER 5

Blame it on the Bogey: The Christian Right's Construction of Homosexuality and the AWARE CSE Programme

Dominic Chua, James Koh and Jack Yong

Introduction

While AWARE's (Association of Women for Action and Research) "old guard" had repeatedly stressed that their Comprehensive Sexuality Education (CSE) package was but one among many programmes, and that it had received disproportionate publicity, the CSE programme was, nonetheless, the focus of an intense war of words in the run-up to the Extraordinary General Meeting (EGM). The Christian-led "new guard" attempted to justify their takeover by charging that the CSE programme was proof that AWARE had taken a "homosexual turn" (*The Straits Times* 24 April 2009a), and that its continued implementation would result in "an entire generation of lesbians" (*The Straits Times* 24 April 2009b). Post-EGM, the CSE programme continued to be a target for a conservative constituency that had previously been galvanised into action by the anti-gay rhetoric of the new guard.

Our chapter examines how the Christian Right in Singapore,[1] as exemplified by Dr Thio Su Mien and the new guard, employed a range of discursive strategies to capture and dictate the terms of public discourse on homosexuality and sexuality education, build a movement against AWARE's CSE programme, and attempt to sway the public's perception on such issues towards their own understanding of sexuality and homosexuality (Thio 2008). Toward this end, moral conservatives spotlighted the issue of homosexuality in AWARE's CSE curriculum,[2] and framed it as a dangerous contagion while, in the ideological contest over AWARE, Thio and her new guard team mobilised support for their cause by evoking fear, anger and disgust toward gay people.

Could the strategies employed by the new guard be better understood in terms of the globalisation of the "family values" movement initiated by the Christian Right in the US? We suggest that rhetorical similarities between the local campaign against AWARE's CSE programme and anti-sexuality education campaigns in the US and Australia are interesting insofar as they are paralleled by links between local Christian Right actors and those on the global stage (see Gibson 2007). Our chapter also examines how the discourse of the Christian Right had an "echo chamber effect", in which key cultural messages travelled beyond the initial circle of influence where they were articulated, and were reproduced in the public domain as "facts". As a result of this echo chamber process, any attempts to contest such messages by supporters of AWARE's CSE programme were stifled, and alternative discourses about homosexuality and sexuality education effectively silenced.

The Dominant Discourse

The words, narratives and symbols used in national debates can shape how we think, talk and feel about major socio-political issues. Firstly, by dictating the terms of debate, one side gains the ability to position its own movement's worldview as common knowledge, and in the process, normalise a particular set of meanings. The side that exercises control of the language and vocabulary used in the discussion of a given issue wields power in determining the parameters of debate (see Foucault 1978; Fairclough 1989). As the sociologist William Gamson (1992) has noted, once a social movement entrenches its own terms in broader public discourse, it becomes very difficult for its opponents to avoid using the same terms, without risking confusion in listeners.

Secondly, words can be used to mobilise people. They persuade the indifferent or the ignorant by appealing to fear and outrage, as seen during the AWARE saga (*The New Paper* 9 May 2009). When a large cohort of likeminded individuals starts to use the same words repeatedly, they can drown out the more timorous voices of their opponents. This visibly (and audibly) happened at the AWARE EGM, and again in online spaces, when conservative protesters flooded Internet forums with anti-gay rhetoric (*TODAY* 5 May 2009).

Our analysis focuses on the rhetorical strategies of the local Christian Right. This is for a compelling reason — while the new guard were fairly reticent about their motives for hijacking AWARE, when one takes into consideration the larger perspective of the public fora, both in print and online media, the Christian Right said more, and said it more loudly. There was a vast disparity in the rhetorical opportunities available to both sides, as opponents to AWARE's CSE had access to a much more culturally powerful repertoire of negative sexual language and images. Janice M. Irvine (2004: 14), an observer of the American cultural wars waged over sexuality education, has noted that:

> Sexuality-aversive language trumps the barely existent language of sexuality affirmation. In matters related to sexuality, it is far easier to accuse than to defend. This is especially true when children are in the picture. The asexual child is a potent symbol whose rhetorical power lies in the appeal of protecting the innocence of the child....

The new guard made such an appeal by highlighting certain information from the trainer's manual of AWARE's CSE programme. While the manual was intended as a loose set of guidelines for the trainers only, the new guard implied that students would be taught the following:

> Anal sex is "healthy or neutral if practised with consent and with a condom".

> [When] using sex toys ... some form of protection [is required], e.g. place a condom over a dildo and clean it as instructed. (*The Online Citizen* 1 May 2009a)

This appeared to be an attempt to spark moral panic and mobilise concerned parents. In turn, it became tricky for those who wished to speak positively of AWARE's CSE or homosexuality to back their views — even if only to say that it is "neutral" — because they could easily be discredited by their conservative detractors. In the US, oppositional rhetorics have, since the sixties, consistently overpowered the responses by sexuality education advocates, who have little available to them, save silence, denials and complicated clarifications (see Irvine 2004). In the Singapore context, where homosexual acts between men are still criminalised under Section 377A of the Penal Code, one could argue that Thio Su Mien and the new guard anticipated correctly that their rhetoric would resonate with, and be amplified by, a broader climate in which homosexuality is bound up with highly negative meanings, including criminality and pathology (Lim 2004).

The Power of Rhetoric

Thio Su Mien and her new guard engaged in the AWARE CSE debate via two major rhetorical modes. The first involves "self-presentation" — how they depicted and cast themselves, wielding certain words to increase their aura of respectability. The second rhetorical mode involves oppositional speech: In such a mode, the conservatives sought to eliminate AWARE's sexuality education programme by associating it with a specific set of negative meanings and flattening the complexity of the subject matter. The discourse framed the particular curriculum as dangerous and depraved — one in which children are taught to think "it's all right to go and experiment with homosexuality, to experiment with anal sex, to experiment with virginity, or the pill or even pre-marital sex", thus playing to historical anxieties about sex (*The Straits Times* 24 April 2009a).

Regarding self-presentation, Thio and her new guard relied heavily on a term very much aligned with the Christian anti-gay movement in the US — "pro-family" (Irvine 2004). When the motives of the takeover by the new guard were first questioned by the public, they positioned themselves as being "pro-women, pro-family and pro-Singapore" (*The Straits Times* 18 April 2009). The term "pro-family" appears innocuous. Few Singaporeans are aware, however, of the term's cultural history — of its use by the Christian Right since the 1970s to condense opposition to a series of social issues, including abortion, homosexuality and sexuality education (Irvine 2004).

Such a rhetorical move was politically astute in three ways. For one, it helped to unite a diverse group of people by couching criticism of AWARE's CSE programme as a defence of Singaporean family values against the incursions of gay equality and the more liberal factions of society (Ministry of Community, Youth and Sports, undated). For another, given the government's own pro-family position in trying to raise the local birth rate, the term imparts a "halo effect", as it taps into the mystique of a governmental imprimatur. Additionally, anyone opposing the agenda of Josie Lau's team could now be tarred as "anti-family", a term with strong negative connotations of social deviance and opposition to stated national policy.

The success of this self-presentation can be seen in the way the local media took up these same terms, and proceeded to frame the ensuing public struggle as one between homosexual groups and "pro-family" groups about sexuality issues (*Channel News Asia* 16 May 2009). Supporters of AWARE's CSE programme as well as members of the gay community, too, were placed on the defensive and forced to take up the Christian Right's terms of reference. Stuart Koe, CEO of the gay portal Fridae.com, when asked to comment in a TV interview, said: "the gay community is pro-family. We have families. We love our families and our families love us" (ibid.).

With regards to the second rhetorical mode, the oppositional speech used by Thio and the new guard can be grouped into several identifiable patterns of discourse. One such pattern involves the use of what we term assumptive language, which takes assumptions about a particular issue as a given fact, even when there is no prior scientific or medical consensus regarding the issue. This enabled them to prey on the fears of many parents and amplify confusion regarding the exact nature of AWARE's CSE programme.

An important example is the oft-repeated claim that homosexuality can be promoted. Josie Lau and some members of her executive committee had joined AWARE because "they had been concerned that the group had a hidden agenda to promote lesbianism and homosexuality as being acceptable" (*The Straits Times* 24 April 2009c). At the 23 April press conference, where Thio Su Mien revealed herself to be the "feminist mentor" of the women behind the takeover, Thio explained how she had felt when she realised AWARE's CSE programme took a "neutral" approach to homosexuality, as opposed to framing it negatively:

> ... I started thinking, "Hey, parents, you better know what's happening," I talked to parents. I said: "You better do something about this; otherwise your daughter will come back and say, 'Mum, I want to marry my girlfriend.' Or your son will say: 'Dad, I want to marry my boyfriend.'" ...The suggestion is that in this programme, young girls from 12 to 18 are taught that it's okay to experiment with each other. And this is something which should concern parents in Singapore. Are we going to have an entire generation of lesbians? (*The Straits Times* 24 April 2009b)

Thio forcefully asserts a causal link between the CSE and a young person's sexual orientation that both wilfully ignores the vast educational, psychological and sociological literature on sexuality education and psychosexual development and flattens the complexity that AWARE's CSE curriculum, in contrast, addressed and communicated (see Savin-Williams 2005). Such a flouting of the most basic rules of reasoned argument — here, a committing of the fallacy of false cause — suggests an eagerness to frighten an ignorant public into consensus with the Christian Right position.

In spite of its relative brevity, the phrase "promotion of homosexuality" accomplishes a tremendous amount of rhetorical work. First, slipping in the assumption that homosexuality *is* promotable to begin with — that people can be "converted" to homosexuality — the term forecloses or blocks any reasoned public discussion about the truth behind its claim. The ideas that homosexuality is a choice, that it can be propagated, that it is contagious, as such, are bundled up and packaged as straightforward and unproblematic "facts", whereas, as noted above, the reality is that the etiology of homosexuality continues to be very much debated.

Second, the phrase forms part of a broader rhetoric of recruitment and conversion that plays to fears of contagion — the notion that children will be converted to homosexuality if there is a growing acceptance of homosexuality in society (Irvine 2004). Thio's comments about AWARE's CSE programme exemplify the use of recruitment rhetoric:

> ... the CSE manual goes further in stating that anal sex can be healthy or neutral with consent and a condom. Not only is this against the law, this kind of "education" is <u>designed to condition the minds of teenage students, from ages 12 to 18, towards the acceptability of homosexuality, purposefully equating homosexuality with the norm of heterosexuality</u>. (Emphasis ours) (*The Straits Times* 18 May 2009)
>
> My concerns were validated when the Ministry of Education (MOE) suspended AWARE's Comprehensive Sexuality Education (CSE) programme, removing AWARE from the external vendors list. The CSE instructors guide contained "explicit and inappropriate" content which conveyed "messages which could <u>promote homosexuality</u>". This violated MOE guidelines that sex education must promote "family values". <u>This proved the presence of the homosexual agenda in our schools for at least two years</u> .... (Emphasis ours) (*The Straits Times* 1 June 2009)

Recruitment rhetoric draws its power by tapping into the anxiety of many parents about what they perceive as the criminality, immorality or merely the social anomaly of being gay. The extent to which these ideas shaped the discussion on AWARE's CSE programme and dictated the terms to be used in the debate can be seen in the way the Ministry of Education (MOE) had to categorically deny that MOE's sexuality programmes, in general, "[do] not promote homosexuality, but [follow] social norms of mainstream society" (Ministry of Education 2009b).

Most significantly, the phrase conflates and collapses two distinct meanings of "promotion". By equating efforts towards non-discrimination of gay persons (a promotion of equality) with the threat-filled notion of "conversion" and "recruitment"[3] as discussed above, the phrase could likely persuade the public to conclude that discrimination towards gays is thereby justifiable, if anything, to protect a whole cohort of defence-less children from turning gay, against their inner-will.

So how did AWARE's old guard respond to the discursive strate-gies deployed by the new guard? At one level, the old guard tried to counter this by focusing on other parts of their CSE programme, and by emphasising that their programme provided "teens with information in a non-judgmental way" (*The Straits Times* 25 April 2009b). They also drew attention to the fact that homosexuality was only covered as part of a two-minute segment. At a broader level, there was a strategic decision on the part of the old guard not to frame the takeover by Thio and her team as a "gay issue". The old guard's understanding of homosexuality in its CSE programme appreciates the complexity of the issue, where:

> ... there is no consensus as to what causes [homosexuality]. What we do know is that many young women suffer in silence and in shame because they fear social ostracism.... In teaching about sexual orientation, we are hoping to dispel myths with accurate information. (Yang 2009)

Yet, rather than mounting a sustained defence of this position, there was a distinct shift towards focusing on the takeover as a hostile intrusion into the secular civil space of a non-governmental organisa-tion (Singam 2009). The government's REACH portal subsequently received 50 comments critical of AWARE's CSE programme, which seems to have had some effect on MOE's decision to tighten controls in the way schools could engage external agencies in conducting sexuality education programmes for their students. The new approval process will now be centralised at MOE, with a more stringent checklist to vet these agencies. The programmes delivered by these agencies will also be audited (Ministry of Education 2009a). It can thus be argued that the public paranoia generated by the local Christian Right's discursive tactics were successful insofar that it led to the government's adoption of a defensive, cautious posture in relation to the content of and manner in which sexuality education is to be conducted in the future.

Contextualising the Discourse

In their book *Globalising Family Values*, authors Doris Buss and Didi Herman examine the increasing engagement of the Christian Right in international politics in its attempt to promote a conservative religious worldview, part of which includes the global "pro-family" movement:

> The American CR [Christian Right] is not simply interested in combating "secular liberalism" on American soil; rather, the CR is intent on both internationalising its domestic concerns and shaping its domestic activism in light of CR global understandings. (Buss and Herman 2003: 15)

Given this global push to dictate the terms by which homosexuality is discussed, it is worth noting that discourse concerning such issues at the national level often echoes the agenda of the Christian Right. This pre-dates the AWARE saga: during the parliamentary debate regarding the repeal of 377A, the part of the Singapore penal code that criminalises sexual activity between men, a key speech against the repeal was by Nominated Member of Parliament Thio Li-Ann, the daughter of Thio Su Mien and a member of the Church of Our Saviour (COOS), a local evangelical church (*The Straits Times* 2 Nov. 2007). Commenting on the issue, Janadas Devan, a newspaper columnist, pointed out that the origins of her speech were derived from the "American religious right" (*The Straits Times* 27 Oct. 2007). In detailing the battles over sex education in the US, Irvine (2004: 73) identifies a number of strategies used by the Christian Right in opposing comprehensive sexuality education:

> …the repetition of evocative sexual language (calling a health education text "pornography"); establishing sex educators as targets for blame (they have been called everything from Communists to dirty

old women to paedophiles); the invention of depravity narratives (circulating fictive tales to scare parents and discredit sex educators); the claim that sex education speech is performative (that talking about sex enacts sex); and the secularisation of religious arguments (using medical claims that may be misleading or inaccurate to advance religious morality).

From the discussion in the preceding section about the new guard's discursive strategies, we see a striking resemblance between their approach and that of the US Christian Right, particularly when we consider the use of certain rhetorical modes and terminology. Such similarities are all the more noteworthy, when we consider the confluence of the following phenomena.

Firstly, other commentators have pointed out that COOS is arguably at the forefront of the anti-gay movement in Singapore with its anti-homosexual initiatives (Hong and Tay 2007; Siew 2009). For example, it houses the Choices Ministry, which claims to help individuals "overcome homosexuality and its related disorders" (Church of Our Savior, undated). The Choices Ministry is in turn associated with Exodus International, which is part of the US conservative and political religious movement (Bancroft 2003).

Secondly, COOS has a number of links to Focus on the Family (FOTF), a US-headquartered organisation known for its extreme evangelicalism and aggressive political lobbing on issues such as sexuality education and homosexuality (Focus on the Family 2008). The chairman of FOTF Singapore, Tan Thuan Seng, is a member of COOS, and a COOS newsletter was noted to have described a FOTF workshop as an opportunity for "outreach" (Hamilton-Hart 2009).

Thirdly, Thio is a member of the COOS, to which Josie Lau and five other members of her executive committee belong to as well.

Finally, during the AWARE debate, COOS' Senior Pastor, Derek Hong, urged his congregation to support Josie Lau's team by voting for them in the EGM, as "there's a line that God has drawn for us, and we don't want our nation crossing that line" (*The Straits Times* 1 May 2009).

While it remains a matter of debate as to how directly the strategies adopted by the new guard were modelled after the US Christian Right, the similarities are undeniable. The new guard's approach should not be viewed in isolation; instead, they are better appreciated when viewed as part of a concerted global effort to introduce conservative religious values into secular political and civil space.

An Echo Chamber Effect

During the AWARE saga, a number of claims were asserted by the new guard, mainly:

(1) Homosexuality threatens (pro) family values (*The Straits Times* 24 April 2009b)

(2) A gay agenda exists (*The Straits Times* 18 May 2009)

(3) Affirmation of homosexuality (within CSE) influences homosexual inclinations amongst children because: (a) homosexuality is promotable (*The Straits Times* 4 May 2009) and (b) it encourages children to experiment with homosexuality (*The Straits Times* 24 April 2009b).

These claims, as embodied in particular terms and phrases and via their reiteration over the full course of the AWARE saga's news coverage, generated an echo chamber effect within the public sphere — an effect wherein "information, ideas or beliefs are amplified or reinforced" by virtue of repetitive communications within an enclosed environment to a point where variations of truths are homogenised and hence perceived as "facts" (Wallsten 2005).

To gauge the echo chamber effect of Christian Right discourse within the local online community, we scanned user comments of three popular local websites, *The Online Citizen*, *Temasek Review* and *Mr Wang Says So*, across the period of the saga. We date this from 12 April, when netizens first questioned the motives behind what they saw as a hostile takeover (*The Straits Times* 12 April 2009), to 21 May, when MOE announced a tightening of controls on sexuality education provided by vendors (*Channel News Asia* 21 May 2009a), as well as its decision to suspend AWARE as a sexuality education vendor (*Channel News Asia* 21 May 2009b).

Articles related to "AWARE" and "homosexual" were retrieved from the websites. We then counted the frequency with which words relating to the Thio's three main assertions (such as "pro-family", "gay agenda" and "children") appeared in the user comments. We did not take into account the contextual meanings behind the use of such words, nor did we account for user-to-user plagiarisms.[4] Our goal in tallying the frequency of these words was simply to obtain a macro-sense of the terms' popularity — regardless of the users' positions on the issues. These terms of reference are significant because they indicate the extent to which the new guard had succeeded in entrenching their discourse, thus generating a ripple effect amongst commentators as they repeated and applied particular terms in their own descriptions and opinions. An online commentator, "Burong" wrote:

> It is appropriate time for <u>pro-family</u> group to take over AWARE [*sic*]. Increasingly, more organisation (including grassroots organisations) are being run by suspect homosexual or singles by choice.... [*sic*] (Emphasis ours) (Choo 2009)

Another commentator, "Right Versus Wrong", noted:

> Now the Government and MOE realises the severity of the situation. How could such lurid and licentious materials be <u>infiltrated in the impressional minds</u> of our next generation? How could AWARE <u>promote</u> these? [*sic*] (Emphasis ours) (*The Online Citizen* 2009b)

As argued earlier, Thio's terms of reference inherently flatten the complexity of the issue. When online users employed these terms, the terms' flattening effect was multiplied and extended beyond their initial reach. Consequently, people might be inclined to take an overly-simplified, moralistic stand on the issue, as the above two quotes illustrate.

Our findings are presented in Figure 1.[5]

We found that discourse amongst the online community focused mostly on the third notion — that homosexuality's inclusion as a topic within an educational setting has a corrupting effect upon young minds. While the above study may not provide an exhaustive understanding of

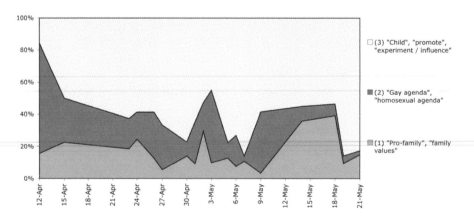

Figure 1. Chronology of the Echo Chamber Effect Amongst Users Across Three Local Websites

how the general public perceived homosexuality, one thing is clear — the local Christian Right had effectively steered public discourse around fears of harming "the romantic child" — a notion coined by historian Anne Higonnet (1998) to explain feelings of emotional apprehensiveness when sexual speech is applied to the young, in a bid to protect their "innocence". Public amplifications of such sentiments serve to fuel public paranoia. Irvine (2004: 13–14) observed that "the romantic child" has long been invoked by the Christian Right in the US:

> Since the initial calls for sex education in the public schools at the turn of the twentieth century, the phantasm of the innocent child being dangerously corrupted by sexual talk has provoked controversy.... Sexual innocence, they claimed, would best be preserved through basic instruction that would thwart the child's sexual curiosity and dampen the imagination. Moreover, these debates over talk versus silence are particularly charged because our determination to preserve the sexually innocent child is infused with such heated emotions.

The invocation of "the romantic child" forms part of the set of oppositional discursive strategies employed by Thio and her team. Similarities between the points raised by Thio and that of western Christian Right counterparts may reflect an alignment between such faith-based groups. The contentious arguments raised were based on the belief that talking about homosexuality at schools could potentially harm the "romantic child" because (a) it leads or influences her to experimentation and (b) since homosexuality is promotable, she is at risk of being influenced into homosexuality. Messages along these lines are powerful, as they speak both to the religiously devout as well as to the secular public.

An online comment posted by "Selena" illustrates these beliefs at work:

> How can such views on anal sex and premarital sex be expressed to our <u>children</u>? It is sickening. Such statements merely give reason for confused kids to feel that they are right to indulge further in such activities. (Emphasis ours) (*The Online Citizen* 2009c)

Public debate on the validity of Thio's charges was scant. Aside from a press conference held on 24 April 2009 to counter the above claims (*The Straits Times* 25 April 2009a), it seemed that the issue of whether Thio's claims held any water was far from the public's mind. As discussed earlier, this could also be due in some part to AWARE's attempt to shift the public's focus away from the issue of homo-sexuality. What seems more plausible to us, however, is the power of the "first mover" — with the Christian Right having established the terms of the debate, there could be little effective questioning of the underlying assumptions behind those terms.

In either case, the words of Thio Su Mien and her team would ripple across socio-political hierarchies. We see this in the language adopted by the government. When government officials decided to speak up about the issues raised by Thio and her team subsequently, similar notions would be "echoed". In describing the motivations behind the AWARE saga, Wong Kan Seng, Singapore's Deputy Prime Minister and then-Minister for Home Affairs, said:

> ... The new Exco members, mentored by veteran lawyer and lay church leader Thio Su Mien, justified their actions by arguing that AWARE had veered towards the <u>promotion of a gay and lesbian agenda</u> in recent years.... (Emphasis ours) (*The Straits Times* 15 May 2009)

Jennifer Chan, press secretary to Singapore's Education Minister Ng Eng Hen, said in a letter to *The Straits Times* on May 7:

> ... Some suggested responses in the instructor guide are explicit and inappropriate, and convey messages which could <u>promote homo-sexuality</u> or suggest approval of premarital sex ... the ministry and its schools "do not <u>promote alternative lifestyles</u> to our students".... (Emphasis ours) (*The Straits Times* 7 May 2009)

On May 22, Education Minister Ng Eng Hen said in an interview with *The Straits Times*:

> ... We do not condone promiscuity, sexual experimentation or <u>promote homosexuality</u>.... (Emphasis ours) (*The Straits Times* 22 May 2009)

Though the above statements, read in their larger context, seem to disprove Thio's claims, they do not question the underlying notion of whether or not homosexuality can be "promoted" in the first place. In fact, by stating that one does not promote homosexuality, that very statement reinforces the public's belief that homosexuality is, indeed, promotable. And by perpetuating the claim that homosexuality is promotable, public fears of its corrupting influence receive further vali-dation — even if one argues that this occurs only incidentally.

Conclusion

It would appear that, in spite of the new guard's losing its takeover bid for AWARE, conservative opponents of the CSE programme have scored an impressive political victory in other domains. By popularising a public vocabulary which framed the CSE as irresponsible and encouraging of deviance, and by linking it to particularly reprehensible stereotypes of the gay community, they have fostered a climate in which all discussion of sexuality education, except of the most conservative variety, has been muzzled. Arguably, they have also succeeded in paralysing an ongoing community debate on the place of gay people in Singapore (*The Straits Times* 15 May 2009).

Our chapter has tried to show how the Christian Right scripted the public conversation on sexuality education through rhetorical frames which organised ambivalence, confusion and anxieties about sexuality into tidy sound bites designed for mass mobilisation. More nuanced and complex understandings of sexuality, such as AWARE's discursive construction of the gay person, cannot help but drop out of this process.

Within the sphere of education, MOE's freeze upon all external sexuality education programmes has narrowed what can be said about sexuality, and will have powerfully signalled to school administrators an official disapproval of any discussion of the issue of homosexuality. Any prior movement towards a greater inclusivity within MOE and its schools would thus have stalled for the moment. In addition, the large majority of schools and teachers would be far more chary about engaging in sexuality education — while it will definitely continue as a programme, teachers will be even less inclined than before to be involved with the programme, and it seems probable that those who do will teach it "defensively", exercising much self-censorship and restraint in the process.

More broadly speaking, the CSE-related component of the AWARE saga demonstrated the existence of local constituencies that can be mobilised by a strategic discourse that fosters the stigmatisation of certain social groups and sexual identities. While the public chiding meted out to the Christian Right by Prime Minister Lee Hsien Loong during his National Day Rally Speech (*Channel News Asia* 16 Aug. 2009) in late August makes such a mobilisation unlikely in the immediate future, the fact that sexuality education and sexuality in general very much remain sites of widespread public ignorance and cultural anxiety opens up the question of whether the Christian Right will again attempt to exploit such volatile sentiments for political gain.

Because sexuality education involves sexual knowledge and citizenship (particularly when the issue of gay persons is raised), it is a matter of wide civic significance. While moral conservatives have managed to dominate the national conversation to date, their success has greatly depended on provocative discursive representations of the gay community that exacerbated public anxieties.

Yet, culture and discourse operate in unpredictable ways. The AWARE debacle saw the emergence of moderate voices, including a moderate Christian constituency (Gwee 2009), which refused to obey the emotional demands that the Christian Right attempted to impose. One might yet take comfort in the thought that when people remain unprovoked by incendiary rhetoric, conservatives run the risk of creating a set of circumstances in which provocative speech casts doubt upon the speakers rather than its targets.

Notes

1. After Buss and Herman, we use the term "Christian Right" (CR) to refer to a broad range of Christian organisations that have tended to form coalitions around an orthodox Christian vision and a defence of the traditional nuclear family formation. Although the CR is by no means monolithic, the term remains a useful category for describing the loose and diverse coalition with which we are concerned. As Buss and Herman note, the term "is essential in characterising [a] very particular relationship between theology and politics" — CR organisations both locally and in the US are "united in a shared opposition to a perceived global liberal agenda, and … [share] a belief in a divinely ordered set of relations within the family, the nation and the church, with each essential to the other" (Buss and Herman 2003: 16).

2. In AWARE's CSE programme, homosexuality is listed as a "neutral issue in an exercise which helps young women understand all the different aspects of their sexuality. The objective of this exercise is to help young women understand that their views are determined by culture, law, mass media, religion, peers and education, amongst others. At no point does the programme try to challenge existing values; it only helps people understand themselves better and be more aware when they take decisions. The ability to rationalise and think through their decisions is one that most parents would want their children to have" (Yang J.Y. 9 April 2009). *AWARE's Comprehensive Sexuality Education Programme*, accessed 6 Sept. 2009, from the We Are AWARE website: <http://www.we-are-aware.sg/2009/

04/09/cse/>. In contrast, the Ministry of Education's Growing Years Package chiefly focuses on the criminalised nature of homosexuality. The key lesson objective is that sexual acts between men constitute a criminal offence in Singapore. It is left to the discretion of the individual school whether to include the topic of homosexuality in their sexuality education programme.

3. Ironically, such concepts are ones with deep resonance within an evangelical Christian cosmology, given the biblical mandate that Christians should seek the conversion of non-believers.
4. A list of limitations to our study can be found in Annex A.
5. Annex A: Table 1a. Frequency at which commonly-used words were cited in user comments.

References

Bancroft, John, 2003, "Can Sexual Orientation Change? A Long Running Saga", *Archives of Sexual Behaviour* 32, 5: 419–68.

Buss, Doris and Herman, Didi, 2003, *Globalising Family Values: The Christian Right in International Politics*. Minneapolis, University of Minnesota Press.

Channel News Asia, 16 May 2009, "Homosexual groups, pro-family groups call for tolerance on gay issue", by Pearl Forss.

————, 21 May 2009a, "MOE tightens control on sex education delivered by external Agencies", by Pearl Forss.

————, 21 May 2009b, "MOE's decision to drop AWARE as external vendor regrettable: AWARE President", by Tan Yew Guan.

————, 16 Aug. 2009, National Day Rally Speech 2009, <http://www.channel newsasia.com/nd09/rally_english.htm#pt6> [accessed 23 Aug. 2009].

Choo Zeng Xi, 2009, "Dr Thio Su Mien's press conference", <http://theonlinecitizen. com/2009/04/dr-thio-su-mien%E2%80%99s-press-conference/> [accessed 6 Sept. 2009].

Church of Our Saviour, undated, "Choices Ministry", <http://www.choices.org.sg> [accessed 6 Sept. 2009].

Fairclough, Norman, 1989, *Language and Power*. London: Longman.

Focus on the Family, 2008, "Counseling for Unwanted Same-Sex Attractions", <http://www.focusonthefamily.com/socialissues/sexual_identity/counseling_ for_unwanted_same_sex_attractions/our_position.aspx> [accessed 1 Sept. 2009].

Foucault, Michel, 1978, *The History of Sexuality, Vol. 1*. New York: Random House.

Gamson, William, 1992, *Talking politics: Comparative Perspectives on Social Movements*. Cambridge: Cambridge University Press.

Gibson, Sally, 2007, "The Language of the Right: Sex Education Debates in South Australia", *Sex Education* 7, 3: 239–50.

Gwee Li Sui, 2009, "Dr Gwee Li Sui's follow up message to his previous rallying call to his fellow Christians", < http://www.sgpolitics.net/?p=2871> [accessed 7 Sept. 2009].

Hamilton-Hart, Natasha, 2009, "Religion, extremism and terrorism: Is there a link?", Paper presented on 2 June at the 23rd Asia Pacific Roundtable, organised by the Institute of Strategic and International Studies (ISIS), Malaysia, <http://www.isis.org.my/files/apr/23rd%20APR/CS1%20-%20Dr. Natasha%20Hamilton-Hart.pdf> [accessed 30 Aug. 2009].

Higonnet, Anne, 1998, *Pictures of Innocence: The History and Crisis of Ideal Childhood*. London: Thames and Hudson.

Hong, Derek and Tay, Shawn, 2007, "God's church & homosexuality", <http://www.coos.org.sg/sermons/files/sermonPDF/200708190830_sermon.pdf> [accessed 31 Aug. 2009].

Irvine, Janice M., 2004, *Talk About Sex: The Battles over Sex Education in the United States*. California: University of California Press.

Lim Kean Fan, 2004, "Where Love Dares (Not) Speak Its Name: The Expression of Homosexuality in Singapore", *Urban Studies* 41, 9: 1759–88.

Ministry of Community Development, Youth and Sports, Singapore, undated, "Families: Introduction", <http://app.mcys.gov.sg/web/faml_main.asp> [accessed 6 Sept. 2009].

Ministry of Education, 2009a, "Information sheet on Ministry of Education's sexuality education (SEd) programme", <http://www.moe.gov.sg/media/press/2009/05/information-sheet-on-ministry.php> [accessed 23 Aug. 2009].

————, 2009b, Forum letter replies, <http://www.moe.gov.sg/media/forum/2009/04/reply-to-media-queries-on-moes.php>[accessed 23 Aug. 2009].

Savin-Williams, R.C., 2005, *The New Gay Teenager*. Cambridge, MA: Harvard University Press.

Siew, Miak, "The Conservative Majority: Examining the Emergence of a Vocal Conservative Minority in Singapore" (unpublished).

Singam, Constance, 2009, "Restore reason, civility to debate", <http://www.we-are-aware.sg/2009/04/28/april-28-%E2%80%93-published-on-st-forum-by-constance-singam-restore-reason-civility-to-debate/> [accessed 31 Aug. 2009].

The New Paper, 9 May 2009, "From ignorance to outrage", by Benson Ang and Han Yongming.

The Online Citizen, 1 May 2009a, "On AWARE's changing slant towards homo-sexuality and Comprehensive Sexual Education in recent years", <http://theonlinecitizen.com/wp-content/uploads/2009/05/aware-cse.pdf> [accessed 23 Aug. 2009].

————, 1 May 2009c, "AWARE's sex education programme — the concerns", <http://theonlinecitizen.com/2009/05/awares-sex-education-programme-the-concerns/> [accessed 6 Sept. 2009].

————, 6 May 2009b, "MOE Statement on Sexuality Education Programme (Updated: Aware's response)", <http://theonlinecitizen.com/2009/05/moe-statement-on-sexuality-education-programme/> [accessed 13 Sept. 2009].

The Straits Times, 27 Oct. 2007, "377A debate and the rewriting of pluralism", by Janadas Devan.

————, 2 Nov. 2007, "A fiery NMP gets her baptism of fire", by Li Xueying.

————, 12 April 2009, "Cyberspace abuzz over AWARE", by Tan Dawn Wei.

————, 24 April 2009a, "Group's agenda 'took gay turn'", by Zakir Hussain.

————, 24 April 2009b, "Lawyer's key role in AWARE coup", by Zakir Hussain.

————, 24 April 2009c, "New exco members tell of death threats", by Sandra Davie.

————, 25 April 2009a, "Old guard members counter allegations of a pro-gay stance", by Sandra Davie and Tan Dawn Wei.

————, 25 April 2009b, "Why neutral stance on homosexuals", by Sandra Davie and Tan Dawn Wei.

————, 1 May 2009, "Church against homosexuality as 'normal alternative lifestyle'", by Nur Dianah Suhaimi.

————, 4 May 2009, "Thio Su Mien's idea of a takeover unravelled".

————, 7 May 2009, "External sex education programmes suspended in schools", by Theresa Tan and Amelia.

————, 15 May 2009, "Exercise restraint, mutual respect, tolerance".

————, 18 May 2009, "Gay activists a key constituency of AWARE" (Forum Page), by Thio Su Mien.

————, 22 May 2009, "MOE tightens vetting of sexuality education", by Theresa Tan.

————, 1 June 2009, "Militant religionism? It's family values" (Forum Page), by Thio Su Mien.

Thio Su Mien, 2008, "Understanding the Homosexual Agenda", in *The Christian Post* (23 Sept.), <http://sg.christianpost.com/dbase/editorial/330/7|15/1.htm> [accessed 23 Aug. 2009].

TODAY, 24 April 2009, "An ugly turn of events; Death threat allegedly received by Exco member", by Zul Othman.

————, 5 May 2009, "Debate still raging in cyberspace; Reach will send feedback to 'relevant Ministries'".

Wallsten, Kevin, 2005, "Blogs and the Bloggers Who Blog Them: Is the Political Blogosphere an Echo Chamber?" Paper presented on 1 September at the annual meeting of the American Political Science Association, <http://www.allacademic.com/meta/p41556_index.html> [accessed 6 Sept. 2009].

Yang J.Y., 2009, "AWARE's Comprehensive Sexuality Education programme", <http://www.we-are- aware.sg/2009/04/09/cse/> [accessed 6 Sept. 2009].

Table 1a. Frequency at which commonly-used words were cited in user comments

Title	Date	URL	(1) "Pro-family", "family values"	(2) "Gay agenda", "homosexual agenda"	(3) "Child", "promote", "experiment/influence"
Takeover of AWARE – "Please sit up and pay attention." (The Online Citizen)	12 April	\<http://theonlinecitizen.com/2009/takeover-of-aware-please-sit-up-and-pay-attention/>	3	13	3
DBS exec is Aware's head (The Online Citizen)	15 April	\<http://theonlinecitizen.com/2009/04/dbs-exec-is-awares-head/>	10	12	22
Dr Thio Su Mien's press conference (The Online Citizen)	23 April	\<http://theonlinecitizen.com/2009/04/dr-thio-su-mien%E2%80%99s-press-conference/>	27	19	45
Leaked emails from COOS members showed that AWARE take-over… (The Temasek Review)	23 April	\<http://temasekreview.com/?p=8185>	7	15	69
AWARE – And Why You Should Cancel Your DBS Credit Cards (Mr Wang Says So)	24 April	\<https://www.blogger.com/comment.g?blogID=4405345292513335071&postID=5151837168724185688>	14	15	28
The crux of the AWARE fiasco is not about homosexuality or religion… (The Temasek Review)	24 April	\<http://temasekreview.com/?p=8272>	27	13	70
Staff sent out email asking members to vote at Aware EOGM (The Online Citizen)	26 April	\<http://theonlinecitizen.com/2009/04/breaking-news-staff-sent-out-emails-asking-members-to-vote-at-aware-ogm/>	14	31	64
MOE rebukes Dr Thio Su Mien's claims about sexuality education in schools (The Temasek Review)	27 April	\<http://temasekreview.com/?p=8493>	1	5	12

Table 1a. continued

Title	URL	Date	(1) "Pro-family", "family values"	(2) "Gay agenda", "homosexual agenda"	(3) "Child", "promote", "experiment/influence"
Aware's sex education programme — the concerns (*The Online Citizen*)	<http://theonlinecitizen.com/2009/05/awares-sex-education-programme-the-concerns/>	30 April	5	8	64
Email sent by Josie Lau's husband, Dr Alan Chin BASHING MOE… (*The Temasek Review*)	<http://temasekreview.com/?p=8604# comments>	30 April	11	4	38
Pastor Derek Hong contradicts himself in his statement on Aware connection (*The Temasek Review*)	<http://temasekreview.com/?p=8652>	30 April	5	1	13
LIVE from Suntec: AWARE EGM, 2 May 2009 (*The Temasek Review*)	<http://temasekreview.com/?p=8732>	1 May	5	6	8
More than a thousand turn up for Aware EOGM (*The Online Citizen*)	<http://theonlinecitizen.com/2009/05/more-than-a-thousand-turn-up-for-aware-eogm/>	1 May	3	16	47
Thio Su Mien asked the crowd to show her some respect during Aware EGM (*The Temasek Review*)	<http://temasekreview.com/?p=8909# comments>	2 May	5	3	9
Aftermath of Aware EGM: Time for some house-keeping (*The Temasek Review*)	<http://temasekreview.com/?p=8931>	3 May	2	9	9
Appeal to Prime Minister on values of marriage and family (*The Temasek Review*)	<http://temasekreview.com/?p=9006>	5 May	4	9	11

(cont'd overleaf)

Table 1a. continued

Title	URL	Date	(1) "Pro-family", "family values"	(2) "Gay agenda", "homosexual agenda"	(3) "Child", "promote", "experiment/ influence"
Catherine Lim's letter to parents on CSE programme (*The Online Citizen*)	\<http://theonlinecitizen.com/2009/05/catherine-lims-letter-to-parents-on-cse-programme/>	5 May	13	8	102
MOE Statement on Sexuality Education Programme (*The Online Citizen*)	\<http://theonlinecitizen.com/2009/05/moe-statement-on-sexuality-education-programme/>	5 May	18	3	119
MOE succumbs to intense lobbying to suspend Aware's CSE (*The Temasek Review*)	\<http://temasekreview.com/?p=9020>	5 May	6	5	18
Supporters of old exco continue to lobby MOE to review Aware's CSE (*The Temasek Review*)	\<http://temasekreview.com/?p=9000>	5 May	2	7	9
The CSE controversy: Let us be guided by pragmatism and scientific evidence (*The Temasek Review*)	\<http://temasekreview.com/?p=9030>	6 May	2	5	19
Sex, Suicide and Poetry (Mr Wang Says So)	\<https://www.blogger.com/comment.g?blogID=4405345292513350718&postID=4595997449522233487>	7 May	10	3	79
Josie Lau removed from her position as Vice President and Head of Marketing, Cards… (*The Temasek Review*)	\<http://temasekreview.com/?p=9147>	9 May	1	11	17

Table 1a. continued

Title	URL	Date	(1) "Pro-family", "family values"	(2) "Gay agenda", "homosexual agenda"	(3) "Child", "promote", "experiment/influence"
Aware saga: Calm down and move on, says DPM Wong Kan Seng (The Online Citizen)	\<http://theonlinecitizen.com/2009/05/aware-saga-calm-down-and-move-on-says-dpm-wong-kan-seng/\>	14 May	26	3	40
Wong Kan Seng sends a stark warning to religious fundamentalists… (The Temasek Review)	\<http://temasekreview.com/?p=9337\>	14 May	2	4	3
Group claiming to represent "conservative majority"… (The Temasek Review)	\<http://temasekreview.com/?p=9507#comments\>	18 May	11	2	15
Sex Education: To Tell or Not to Tell (Mr Wang Says So)	\<https://www.blogger.com/comment.g?blogID=4405345292513335071&530471406567712579&pli=1\>	19 May	2	1	18
Dr Ng Eng Hen's revised approach to sex education in schools fair and balanced (The Temasek Review)	\<http://temasekreview.com/?p=9636#comments\>	21 May	19	3	104
Total			255 16.52%	234 15.16%	1,055 68.33%

Notes:
1. Only user comments were counted. Text from the main article were not considered.
2. The numbers above are based purely on word count. Context, plagiarism and repeat postings were not taken into consideration.
3. We recognise that some words will inadvertently appear more frequently due to the nature and content of the main article — the appearance of the word "child" in an article about education, for instance. However, we also noticed that there was a strong tendency for many of the user comments to go off-tangent from the main article, e.g. user comments about 377A in an article about the takeover.
4. Spelling errors and synonyms were not taken into consideration for this word count.
5. We note that the reader profile of each website may be subject to the site's own editorial direction.

CHAPTER 6

The Role of the Media: Investigative Journalism in Singapore

Loh Chee Kong

Introduction

Once in a while, a great story comes along and for the journalists in Singapore, the AWARE (Association of Women for Action and Research) saga, even in its initial stages, had all the right ingredients — the controversial issues of homosexuality and religion, a covert plot, a bitter power struggle and a cast of relatively well-known figures — to become a blockbuster. Apart from the reams of newspapers devoted to the saga, it also took on a life of its own on the Internet, spawning numerous online discussions and commentaries by amateur journalists. But perhaps more than anything else, the AWARE episode was a poignant reminder of the media's ability to mobilise public opinion, a salient trait often warned against in politically-sterile Singapore. How else could one account for a turn-out of more than 3,000 Singaporeans and non-Singaporeans alike at the AWARE extraordinary meeting (EGM) on 3 May 2009, a number of whom had previously scant idea of its work as an NGO? How else could one explain the strong views held by those in attendance, with many taking sides as the war of words between the two factions was played out in both the mainstream media and the Internet?

The EGM was, in every sense, extraordinary. It was a throwback to the heady pre-independence years, when newspapers were regularly used to not just shape public opinion but also get people out of their houses and act on it. In a country where it is constantly made clear to media practitioners that they do not set the political agenda, the Singapore government naturally frowned upon the rare demonstration of investigative journalism that brought the AWARE saga to light, which, to some observers, even bordered on "crusading journalism". Apart from examining the tone and tenor of the media coverage, this chapter would also explore the circumstances leading to the rare demonstration of investigative journalism, at least in the Singapore context, in civil society in 2009. And in contrast to previous examples of investigative journalism — most notably with the National Kidney Foundation saga in 2005, when investigative journalism was lauded for unearthing unethical practices — why did the government voice its disapproval on more than one occasion of the media coverage, apart from the fact that it had involved the sensitive topic of religion?

Any attempt to understand the role that the mainstream media played in the AWARE saga should be framed by the political expectations of the media. In what was a defining speech on the ruling People's Action Party's (PAP) stance on the role of the Singapore media, then Deputy Prime Minister Lee Hsien Loong said in 2004 that the media was expected to play a "constructive role in nation building". Adding that the Singapore media model must be distinct from its American counterpart, "which uses its powerful position to set the national agenda, champion policies and pass judgment on the country's leaders", Lee reiterated that the Singapore media should "adopt a national perspective on issues" and "avoid crusading journalism, slanting news coverage to campaign for personal agendas" (*The Straits Times* 7 Jan. 2004). As the dust settled on the AWARE saga, the media, in particular, *The Straits Times*, were roundly criticised publicly in Parliament by a couple of Members of Parliament (MPs), taking the cue from Deputy Prime Minister Wong Kan Seng who, in response to media queries, described the coverage as "excessive and not sufficiently balance"; and also "extensive and even breathless" (*The Straits Times*; *TODAY* 15 May 2009). At the National Day Rally some three months after the saga, PM Lee brought up the episode again (*TODAY* 17 Aug. 2009), and was critical of the media coverage which not only set the stage for a fierce public debate but also invariably stoked the flames of what Lee described as "a sensitive matter where views are deeply divided". The manner in which the saga unfolded also risked spilling over into relations between the different religions, Lee noted.

But while government voices were unanimous in criticising the media coverage, the views on the ground were mixed: with those sympathetic to the so-called "old guard" of AWARE expressing support for the coverage while those who were rooting for the other camp were vehement in their protest against it. Judging by letters from the public to the newspapers, criticisms outnumbered support of the media coverage. However, such a measurement might not be representative of ground sentiments; similarly, the more extensive and sympathetic media coverage of the old guard of AWARE by the mainstream media and socio-political websites such as *The Online Citizen*, should not be seen as reliant measure of public support for either camps. But one thing is for sure, public opinion was split.

Analysing the Coverage

The heavy criticisms in Parliament by MPs saw *Straits Times* editor Han Fook Kwang make the rare move of publicly defending the broadsheet's coverage of the saga (*The Straits Times* 30 May 2009). *The Straits Times* had broken the story (*The Straits Times* 10 April 2009) that a group of "unknowns" had abruptly, albeit legitimately, taken over the office at AWARE. The article explicitly suggested that the leadership grab was an orchestrated coup and insinuated heavily the new executive committee's anti-homosexuality stance, by pointing out that one of the members of the new guard had voiced her displeasure at a petition to repeal Section 377A of the Penal Code which criminalises homosexual sex between consenting men.

The article also pointed out that two other supporters had written to the newspaper in their personal capacity to caution against the risks of promoting the homosexual lifestyle. In a 2,000-word article, Han reiterated that the "curious situation" as a result of the takeover had invited press scrutiny, especially when the new guard members were "unwilling to explain who they were, why they had acted and what they intended to do with AWARE". Taking issue with MP Sin Boon Ann's criticism that the press was "framing this episode as one that carries a religious undertone", Han insisted that from the outset, the newspaper had to do its own research given the reticence of the new guard members. Han wrote:

> Our checks showed one common link initially: several members of the new group had written letters to the press expressing concern about the perils of promoting a homosexual lifestyle in Singapore.

We subsequently also found out that several of them belonged to the same Anglican Church of Our Saviour. We reported these factually. (*The Straits Times* 30 May 2009)

While Han suggested that the same press scrutiny would have been accorded should a similar leadership grab had occurred in any other "society, grassroots organisation, union, clan or country club", it would be safe to assume that the reporter who broke the news had already had some inkling by then of what was brewing behind the scenes (even though, as the newspaper took pains to point out, it was only at the new guard's press conference that it learnt of the fact that senior lawyer Dr Thio Su Mien had urged them to challenge AWARE's leadership because of concerns over its alleged homosexual leanings).

And whether intentionally or otherwise, through purposeful reporting or simplistic public reading, the angle of the coverage was cast as a group of overzealous Christians — unhappy with the liberal attitudes of the old guard — had orchestrated a coup at one of Singapore's most influential NGOs. Undoubtedly, the members of the new guard did themselves no favour by what can only be described as a public relations disaster. More often than not, dignified silence only works when the party under siege has established a certain credibility. And as far as the credibility stakes were concerned, the old guard won hands down given the prominence of their members, which included well-known women activists, former journalists and a former Nominated Member of Parliament.

The clout of the old guard and its cosy relationship with media practitioners in the newsrooms through years of cooperation also gave them greater access to the media, which it duly used to its advantage. Within one month when the story broke, *The Straits Times* generated an average of more than one article daily, including *Sunday Times* spread (*The Straits Times*' Sunday edition) in which former AWARE presidents Constance Singam and Nazar aired unfettered criticisms of the new guard (*Sunday Times* 19 April 2009).

While several of the protagonists were former *Straits Times* journalists, Han reiterated that the newspaper had acted on a tip off. It was not until it became apparent that there were underlying issues behind the leadership grab, that *TODAY* — in line with its founding philosophy of being an issue-based newspaper — got in on the act as well.

The free sheet, which had to play catch up on the story, consciously took a more detached approach, focusing on the issues (including

AWARE's sexuality education programme in schools) and not on the personalities — a practical approach given its manpower limitations.

In *The Straits Times'* defence, Han stressed that the new guard was always given the right of reply but they chose to remain silent, a charge disputed by the new guard members who insisted they were merely just following protocol. Cutting to the bone, the new guard had under-estimated the power of the mass media and the importance of good public relations. While many of them were from the corporate sector, few — with the exception of new guard member Lois Ng, a former *Straits Times* journalist, and Lau, who headed DBS Bank's marketing team for cards and unsecured loans — had previous experience with the media, much less in crisis communication. Having said that, the thought of accidentally revealing its covert plot must have weighed heavily on the minds of the new guard in deciding how to engage the media and resulted in the mistaken belief that the less said, the better.

The nature of a news vacuum is such that it invites speculation, which would then spiral out of control. On hindsight, the new guard must have rued its oversight in failing to come up with a media engage-ment plan.

Ironically, *The Straits Times* had also invited scrutiny on itself by straying from accepted practices in most newsrooms, plausibly due to a considered stance by its senior editors to exploit the initiative it held over its rivals, both in the mainstream and on the Internet. For example, in Singapore where "crusading journalism" is frowned upon by the powers-that-be, it is an unwritten rule for editors to relieve reporters who appear to become too involved in a story, if only to avoid being seen as pursuing an agenda. *The Straits Times* coverage was largely driven by its senior writer who had broken the story, prompting criticisms from some quarters that he was known to be sympathetic to gay causes. While not everyone agrees with the role of "crusading journalism", such a self-imposed practice also prevents a newspaper's coverage from inadvertently taking on a subjective slant — given that reporters are human and susceptible to taking sides, despite the sacrosanct value of journalistic objectivity. And even on occasions when a seasoned journalist can be trusted to exercise objecti-vity, newspapers are extremely mindful of public perception. Given the close relationship between the Singapore media and the govern-ment, the last thing editors want is for a journalist to be perceived as driving his or her own agenda.

As such, newspapers not only have to be unbiased, they must be seen to be so. While editors recognise the benefits of having a "specialist" journalist, given his access to contacts and background knowledge, on a particular issue, particularly in a story with fast-changing developments, they would deliberately take the journalist "out of the heat" (in newsroom lingo) from time to time. It is for this political reason that they usually make a conscious decision to involve more than one journalist from the onset, apart from sharing the work-load. To put it simply, the "specialist" journalist, while still being active in the coverage, should not be helming it.

Furthermore, it is common understanding among newsmen that a party's failure to respond to media questions does not give a newspaper *carte blanche* to publish unverified allegations and unsubstantiated criticisms against it, particularly from an opposing party with an obvious agenda to discredit it. In order to exercise its position of influence responsibly, editors have to seek out counterviews to balance the coverage. In the case of the AWARE saga, *The Straits Times* should have sought comments from supporters of the new guard or more neutral comments from observers, to work around the protracted silence from the new guard. By focusing on the individuals, *The Straits Times* also needlessly framed them as "heroes" and "foes", distracting readers from the real issues at hand, including the proper limits for religious activism. On their part, journalists also have to uphold their professionalism in spite of their personal allegiance or beliefs — a professional code of conduct they should have been constantly reminded before they were sent out on their assignments.

While there could also be a natural bias among reporters (given the tendency for the industry to attract individuals with more liberal attitudes), it was regrettable that some reporters were seen embracing members of the old guard following their return to office after the EGM; a MediaCorp news reporter could barely hide her glee on tele-vision. In this aspect, Singapore's media organisations have ample grounds for self-review in their strive for excellence.

Still, it was clear that *The Straits Times* emerged the winner in the readership stakes, with readers keenly following its comprehensive and extensive coverage of the saga, never mind the fact that *TODAY* was able to claim the moral high ground. Try as it might, *TODAY* could not wrestle ownership of the coverage from *The Straits Times*. While it managed to stand out with its coverage of the controversy over the sexuality education programme, on hindsight, it was unable to do so on other pertinent issues — including religious activism, governance of NGOs and corporate interference in the NGO sector — with its hit-and-run type of coverage.

A Triumph for Investigative Journalism

As Han had noted, the media's "breathless" coverage could be attributed to the many twists and turns as the saga unfolded. Apart from the leadership takeover, AWARE's new president, Claire Nazar, resigned suddenly without explanation within a fortnight. Her replacement, Josie Lau, was then criticised publicly by her employer DBS Bank for taking office. Soon after, concerns over AWARE's sexuality education programme and its instructors' guide also surfaced eventually, with the programme eventually suspended (*The Straits Times* 7 May 2009). But that is only one side of the story.

In terms of news value alone, the AWARE saga deserved the extensive coverage — although some have taken issue with its tone. In his reply to media queries, DPM Wong stressed that the episode was "surely not the most important challenge facing Singapore", although there were "important issues at stake" (*The Straits Times*; *TODAY* 15 May 2009). Nevertheless, if the heated public debate over Section 377A in 2007 was anything to go by, the AWARE saga simply drove home the point that, together, religion and homosexuality was a hot-button issue among many Singaporeans. Some would argue that this alone justified the extensive coverage, particularly when it did not come at the expense of any other more newsworthy happening at that time.

As far as the media is concerned, the episode gave newsrooms the rare opportunity to determine the news flow and, to a large extent, set the agenda, given the government's decision not to intervene overtly. Not only was this the biggest news during an exceptionally dry news month (traditionally dominated by post-Budget news and Committee of Supply debates, both of which had been brought forward this year), this was also one of the rare occasions when the media had a free rein. On hindsight, the media was never going to let the saga slip away that easily. But more than just that, editors at rival media companies MediaCorp and Singapore Press Holdings were eager to seize the initiative and not cede new grounds on an episode that had griped the general population, especially at a time when the media was facing the double whammy of economic downturn and declining readership, with the latter partly attributed to the growth of online news sources.

Given its faster turnaround time and fewer levels of gatekeepers at the expense of multiple layers of fact checking, the online media has gradually emerged as a competitor to the mainstream media, pipping the latter to breaking news on a few occasions. The AWARE saga presented a golden opportunity for the mainstream media to re-exert its authority as the Number One source for news, thus also raising the stakes further for the rival media organisations, somewhat escalating to a situation where the winner takes all. Reporters were instructed to constantly keep tabs on the developments and, at the height of the saga, they were churning out on average of at least one article per day. The overwhelming media turnout at the press conference held by the new guard led by Lau on 23 April 2009 underscores the point which is comparable to those witnessed in the past only at events of great national significance.

As far as irony goes, what began as press scrutiny on the AWARE takeover resulted in scrutiny on the press, particularly its role in the development of Singapore's nascent civil society. Still, opinions are split over whether the vociferous manner in which the saga played out was desirable to that end. But the Prime Minister made his stance clear during the National Day Rally (*TODAY* 17 Aug. 2009): It was "hardly the way to conduct a mature discussion of a sensitive matter where views are deeply divided". It is anyone's guess whether the manner in which the saga played out would influence the government in the way it deals with future upheavals in the civil society.

With its powers to galvanise citizens into action, a vibrant media lies at the heart of any healthy civil society. Yet, given the government's emphasis on harmony and consensus, the media, as compared to its Western counterpart, is working within a tight space even as it aligns itself to the government's stated objective to encourage "the development of civic society and gradual widening of the OB markers", in the words of DPM Wong (*The Straits Times*; *TODAY* 15 May 2009). As DPM Wong noted, the government "will not stand by and watch when intemperate activism threatens our social fabric" (*The Straits Times*; *TODAY* 15 May 2009). While it may seem that the Singapore media is caught between a rock and a hard place, the coverage of the AWARE saga emphatically underlines the importance of its commitment to a robust public sphere. For all the flak that *The Straits Times* received, one thing is certain: The intentions of Lau's team would never have come to light had it not been for its rare display of investigative journalism.

Conclusion

As far as the Singapore mainstream media was concerned, the AWARE saga provided a reality check not just for the news organisations but also for the government, which has kept a tight rein on the media. For the news organisations, the episode was a good test of how they should go about conducting investigative journalism into the taboo area of religion, in particular, religious activism which is expected to rise in the near future. The media had predominantly framed the issue as a tussle between two groups (which inadvertently led to accusations of biasness), in contrast to framing it as a case of a group of religious followers seeking to challenge Singapore's secularism by imposing their views through an NGO.

Any notion that the government would incur significant political cost by interfering with the AWARE coverage appears misguided. It is not beyond the government to nip the issue in the bud — either overtly or behind closed doors — should it feel necessary to do so. With the saga playing itself out — with minimal government intervention — the episode was a test case in providing a glimpse into how the media in the Internet era could mobilise public opinion. It was a vivid demonstration of the power of the mainstream media, multiplied several folds by the Internet. Undoubtedly, the saga holds many lessons as the government ponders over its approach to manage and utilise both the mainstream and online media. Unfortunately for advocates of greater press freedom, one of the most abiding lessons for the government could be the need to retain its hold over the mainstream media — even more so in the New Media age.

References

The Straits Times, 7 Jan. 2004, "I have no doubt our society must open up further", by Lee Hsien Loong.

————, 10 April 2009, "Unknowns knock out veterans at Aware polls", by Wong Kim Hoh.

————, 7 May 2009, "External sex education programmes suspended in schools", by Theresa Tan and Amelia Tan.

————, 15 May 2009, "Exercise restraint, mutual respect, tolerance", by Wong Kan Seng.

————, 30 May 2009, "Why we covered Aware saga the way we did", by Han Fook Kwang.

The Sunday Times, 19 April 2009, "Constance Singam quits as Aware adviser; Three-time president describes her unhappiness with the new team in a letter to long-time members", by Wong Kim Hoh.

_____, 19 April 2009. "Claire Nazar: Why I quit as Aware president", by Serene Goh.

TODAY, 15 May 2009, "Media coverage 'not sufficiently balanced' at times", by Zul Othman.

_____, 17 Aug. 2009, "Time to turn down the 'amplifiers'", by Loh Chee Kong.

CHAPTER 7

Strength in Diversity: Organisational Lessons from the AWARE Saga

Alex Tham[1]

Introduction

The engineered takeover of AWARE's (Association of Women for Action and Research) executive committee and the subsequent victory of the so-called "old guard" over the "new guard" raised the important question about what form democracy should take in Singapore. This does not have an easy answer. On the other hand, there seemed to be no question why Thio Su Mien and her group of fellow church members could so easily take over AWARE's executive committee (Exco). *The Straits Times* pointed out that AWARE's old guard had become too "complacent". To prevent another hostile takeover, it was recommended that AWARE implement stricter membership criteria in its Constitution and improve its leadership interaction with the rank-and-file (Low and Au Yong 2009).

This recommendation, however, assumed that AWARE had an *hierarchical* organisational structure with vertical relations between leaders and subordinate members. In such hierarchies, improved communication between ranks merely reinforces the members' dependence on their leaders. However, AWARE's structure is more horizontally organised, with "relatively loose, informal and decentralised" (Rucht 1996: 188) relations between members. In this *network* form of organisation, members and leaders are interdependent and "engaged in reciprocal, preferential, mutually supportive actions" (Powell 1990: 303). Access to resources is more open in network organisations, and ordinary members have greater freedom to take charge of their own projects.

The culture of an organisation is linked to its form. This is evident when one looks at the different meanings of conflict in vertical and horizontal relations. In hierarchical organisations, action tends to be instrumental. The most efficient means are directed towards clearly defined ends. Conflict in this context is unproductive and perceived as a deviation from the norm. To prevent such deviations, hierarchical organisations place a premium on homogeneity. Norms are legitimised among subordinates through authority from above, and those who do not conform are excluded. On the other hand, network forms of organisation are inclusive and derive their strength from diversity. Within a relatively flat organisational structure, action tends to be value-driven. Unlike hierarchical organisations where norms are taken for granted, the plurality of perspectives in network organisations subject values to contestation and increase the likelihood of conflict. But this conflict does not weaken the organisation. Instead, its resolution through negotiation and deliberation unites disparate members together such that the organisation as a whole becomes stronger (Simmel 1955). Even so, diversity is not eradicated. Instead, a common understanding emerges that forms the basis for future contestations and growth. This productive tension between "co-existing logics and frames of action" increases the organisation's long-term adaptability (Girard and Stark 2003).

Diversity, however, can be a source of weakness as well as strength. Paradoxically, it was AWARE's pluralism that made it vulnerable to a hostile takeover. Much like how Western liberal democracies provide the space for anti-social groups to flourish, AWARE's inclusiveness enabled several of its members to form a group premised on exclusion. If this group had been successful in its takeover bid, it might have radically transformed the organisation. This time around, AWARE's network and the social capital it generated proved more resilient. This raises the question of how voluntary associations like AWARE can safeguard their diversity without compromising the structure on which their pluralism is based. This chapter examines the organisational structure of AWARE and explores the importance of diversity and conflict to the NGO as well as the social capital it was able to generate in times of crisis.

Diversity and Conflict

AWARE's diversity is premised on its guiding principle of equality for all women. The backdrop to the founding of AWARE in December 1985 was the 1983 National Day Rally speech, when Prime Minister Lee Kuan Yew contrasted the higher birth rates among less-educated women against the lower rates among educated women. Subsequently, the government came up with a "Graduate Mothers Priority Scheme" in 1984 that offered married women with five "O"-Level passes up to S$10,000 in tax relief for each of their first three children if they had their third child by 28 years of age. Furthermore, their children would be given primary school placement benefits. At the same time, low-income and less-educated married women under 30 years of age would be given S$10,000 if they underwent sterilisation after their first child (Saw 2005: 145–56). This controversial policy generated a fierce response from Singapore society and was eventually withdrawn a year later. AWARE's founders, in particular, took offence at the government's unquestioned ascription of a woman's role to the domains of wife and mother. Women deserved the right to choose who they wanted to be and AWARE was established to empower them to do so.

Behind this broad agenda for equal gender opportunities lay a specific concern for class inequalities along educational differences, particularly among minority Malay and Indian women (Lyons 2007: 85–93). From early on AWARE made a concerted effort to reach out across class and ethnic boundaries. Membership-wise, AWARE has always been ethnically diverse. This is evident from the ethnic composition of the AWARE executive committee and sub-committees. Both young and elderly women are also viewed as important groups. AWARE has had several sub-committees looking at issues pertinent to these two age groups.

In terms of social class, AWARE's membership is mostly comprised of highly-educated women who work in the skilled and managerial sector. In 1996, women from the professional and administrative fields comprised around 61 per cent of AWARE's total membership (see Figure 1). Homemakers, production and clerical staff comprised just under a third.[2]

Nevertheless, the projects that AWARE has been involved in over the years clearly indicate attempts to reach out to less-educated and lower-income groups. Free legal clinics, a telephone helpline, and project groups addressing issues that concern disenfranchised women,

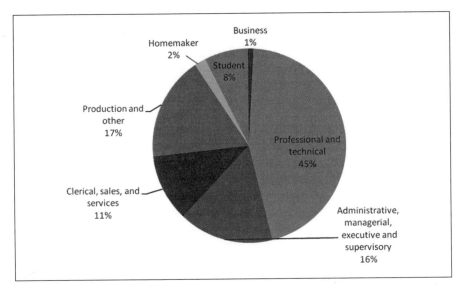

Source: Membership records taken from Rodan, 1996.

Figure 1   Occupational Distribution of Membership

such as education, HIV/AIDS, rape and family violence, have all been part of AWARE's work. Since 1998 AWARE has had a sub-committee that researches and writes "shadow papers" on the status of women in Singapore for the UN Convention on the Elimination of all forms of Discrimination Against Women (CEDAW). So far, AWARE has submitted two shadow reports, the latest in May 2007, which substantially increases the scope and analysis of the reports written by the Singapore government.

AWARE's diverse outreach across class, ethnicity, age and other social categories is therefore not merely a residual function of its activities to promote gender equality. On the contrary, pluralism is a core organisational value around which its members' actions are oriented. During the takeover saga, the boundaries of AWARE's diverse constituency was challenged on two fronts. First, whether AWARE should include homosexuals in its call for gender equality. Second, whether AWARE should adopt a more inclusive membership for men. After a press conference on 23 April 2009, *The Straits Times* reported that Josie Lau's group and their "feminist mentor" Thio Su Mien had expressed concern that AWARE's agenda had taken a gay turn. Thio also found, to her "horror", that AWARE had considered giving male members voting rights at a 2008 AGM. In response, a former AWARE leader, Kanwaljit Soin, said that "[AWARE] cannot condemn, deny or exclude any woman because of her sexual orientation." Soin also stated that she believed AWARE "cannot change the world for women until we bring the men onboard". Nevertheless, she clarified that the motion to give men voting rights had been defeated at the 2008 AGM (Boon 2009).

These conflicts over the scope of AWARE's inclusiveness should not be seen as one-off incidences unique to the takeover period, but as an integral part of managing diversity in the organisation. As members bring their differing views to the table, even pluralism can come under interrogation. Take for instance the "Blueprinter Controversy". In 1995, a sub-committee came up with a feminist blueprint that would "provide a means to chart future directions [for AWARE] by providing signposts and reference points to members and the leadership" (Lyons 2007: 114). The paper was rejected at an extraordinary general meeting in July 1995. The interesting aspect of this Blueprint debate was that it was centered around the meaning of "feminism" in AWARE. At a general level AWARE's activism for gender equality constitutes a form of feminism, and several AWARE stalwarts have identified themselves as feminists (Singam 2007). Nevertheless, as AWARE President Dana Lam-Teo told me, there are many interpretations of feminism and the label's radical connotations have made many modern Singaporean women averse against calling themselves feminists (Dana Lam-Teo, pers. comm.). As such, any feminist programme for AWARE's members had to accommodate its plurality of meanings and the social context. According to AWARE founding member Margaret Thomas, there was a sense among some of the AWARE stalwarts that the Blueprinters were "young members steeped in academic thinking [that was] too ideological" (Margaret Thomas, pers. comm.). To the Blueprinters' shock, some members even "insisted that AWARE was not and had never been a 'feminist' organisation" (Lyons 2007). This episode in AWARE's history is a reminder that even core organisational values, such as those signified by the label "feminism", is subject to contestation between members. More importantly, it also shows that AWARE's commitment to diversity is in itself a safeguard against radicalism within the group, since its members, by and large, will seek a common middle ground through deliberation.

In contrast to the old guard's emphasis on open interaction, however, the relations among the members of the new guard were strengthened through exclusion. The boundary that the new guard established to distinguish themselves from the old guard was evident at the March 2009 AGM, where at least 80 of the attendees were new members who had joined earlier in the year. This influx was more than twice the average attendance of an AWARE AGM. Dana Lam-Teo observed that "there were many faces I had not seen before…. In previous years, even if there were new members, they would be known to one or more of the older members" (Wong 2009a). These new members had come in support of the new guard and duly voted them in. They were not interested in interacting with the other AWARE members nor were they immediately concerned about AWARE's outreach to wider society, since their activism was directly focused on the internal reform of the organisation.

Whereas the old guard viewed conflict as a form of deliberation and thus potentially unifying, conflict for the new guard was essentially political and divisive. The boundary established by the new guard therefore separated AWARE into two distinct camps. Unlike the multiplicity of different groups supported by the earlier organisational structure, an AWARE member was now either a "friend" or "enemy" depending on which side of the boundary she stood on (Schmitt 2007). This was not a mere symbolic distinction, but was manifested in real action through incidences like the changing of the locks at AWARE's offices (Tan 2009b), the exclusion of a veteran Exco member at a press conference organised by the new guard (Basu 2009), and the sudden expulsion of the chair of AWARE's CEDAW sub-committee (*The Straits Times* 2009a).

It is important to recognise that the new guard's friend/enemy distinction was crucial to its own identity. By establishing a boundary that separated them from "the other", the members of the new guard strengthened the ties between themselves and other like-minded women. The different types of relations that emerge from diversity or homogeneity create vital sources of social capital for AWARE. The rest of this chapter will elaborate on how AWARE's particular organisational structure was able to mobilise resources precisely because of its commitment to pluralism and equality, and why this structure was also susceptible to a takeover attempt.

Social Capital and Organisational Structure

Social capital is a specific resource that accumulates when an individual is embedded in a group or network of mutually acknowledged relationships. Such relationships can be formed through kinship, religion, friendship, work, and shared social categories like ethnicity and class. The social capital that accrues may be "converted" into economic capital, much like the *guanxi* relations that Chinese businesses are known for. But social capital can also be a source of mobilisation, like how a person relies on friends to help out in a project. In this regard, the outcome of social capital not only depends on the size of the group, but also on the resources that the group possesses (Bourdieu 1986: 249).

It is important to distinguish the outcomes of social capital from its sources and structural conditions. With regard to the AWARE takeover, there were two sources of social capital: bounded solidarity and enforceable trust (Portes 1998: 7–9). The social capital that emerges out of bounded solidarity is value-driven and involves a mutual recognition of a common identity. The consciousness shared by many AWARE members, of being part of a community of women campaigning for equality, was a form of bounded solidarity. On the other hand, social capital can also be a product of enforceable trust. In this case, the motivation is largely instrumental. There is the expectation of something in return, and a powerful sense of accountability to the group as a whole that enforces trust and minimises defections.

The differences between social capital from bounded solidarity and social capital from enforceable trust are intricately linked to organisational structure. At the same time as the new guard's group identity was premised on its exclusion of the AWARE old guard, ties within the new guard itself were strengthened by the joint membership they had with the same church. At least six members of the new guard belonged to the same church (Tan 2009a). Thio's leadership status among the church-goers was replicated within the new guard in AWARE. The new guard team centered around Thio was premised on enforceable trust. Unlike NGOs where solidarity emerged from shared values, the source of the new guard's social capital was trust enforced by the mutual awareness of the costs of defection. Although the actions of the new guard were justified by a specific Christian notion of the ideal family, the hierarchical structure of the new guard enforced homogeneity and imposed sanctions on defections. This stood in stark contrast to liberal NGOs with flat network structures, where members could participate in multiple projects freely with less fear of sanction.

This difference between enforceable trust and trust based on shared values explains why the new guard could conduct a hostile takeover of AWARE. First let us look at how solidarity emerged out of the old group's organisation of AWARE. The strength of AWARE was its ability to reach out and draw on the resources of diverse groups based on its premise of gender equality for all women. Ironically, this strength emerged out of a particular difficulty that AWARE faced. Despite having social services such as a helpline and legal clinics in place, AWARE is not a social work organisation. It is primarily research-driven and its members are mostly educated English-speaking women with social backgrounds that set them apart from Singapore's "heart-landers". According to Margaret Thomas, this made AWARE vulnerable to criticisms of being elitist, but AWARE "makes no apologies" for its emphasis on research (Margaret Thomas, pers. comm.). Instead, AWARE serves as a resource hub where knowledge is distributed outwards in the form of policy recommendations against institutional gender bias.

From interviews with AWARE leaders and volunteers, I found that the organisation's workflow process hinged on an open network of weak ties to diverse segments of society. Moreover these weak ties were also *sources* of information flowing into the organisation. AWARE's helpline is one example. The main purpose of the line is to provide on-the-spot counseling for women. Lines are staffed by trained personnel who listen and talk through whatever problems are troubling the women at the other end. However, the helplines are also resources for research. While the names and identities of the callers are strictly con-fidential, information about growing issues of concern among Singa-porean women, such as spousal abuse, can still be obtained from the volume of calls. From this information, projects are drawn up for issues that have not yet been publicly addressed.

AWARE's outreach activities create a virtuous cycle where women keen to tap AWARE's network become members, thereby bringing their own knowledge and social networks with them into the organisation. Dana Lam-Teo recounted to me that she had joined AWARE through the recommendation of her friend, Constance Singam. Dana had been concerned about the state of education for women in Singapore, and Constance, a former AWARE Exco member, suggested that she submit a proposal to AWARE and chair a sub-committee to conduct focus group studies on the issue (Dana Lam-Teo, pers. comm.). Separately, another volunteer I spoke to wanted to set up a group promoting awareness of sexual harassment against women in Singapore. She was in the process of discussing a project with AWARE not only because she knew it would be supportive, but also to tap on its resources.

This circulation of information and resources is facilitated by AWARE's relatively flat organisational structure. Volunteers who have a project in mind can approach other AWARE members with a proposal. The scope and area of focus is discussed, a sub-committee is formed, and AWARE contributes resources for research. Once a paper is written, it is meant to be actionable. Its contents are put to a vote and, if accepted, AWARE liaises with government agencies and non-government organisations to put it into effect. After the issues are brought to public awareness, new organisations might branch out of AWARE to better dedicate resources to the specific issue. The Center for Promoting Alternatives to Violence (PAVe), for instance, was set up after AWARE raised the issue of family violence.

Through these processes of research, deliberation and action, ties are built and a sense of bounded solidarity emerges among AWARE members and volunteers. As mentioned earlier, conflict is an integral part of the management of diversity in AWARE. Just as the first president of AWARE, Lena Lim, was chosen because she "embodied the politically acceptable combination of a wife, mother and career woman" (Lyons 2007: 91), AWARE's conflict resolution process tends towards the largest common denominator of Singapore women. To more radical elements, this might appear conservative. But it is also an important unifying process and can mobilise a diverse network of otherwise dissimilar women.

However, the weakness of diversity is the general tendency of people to mix with those similar to themselves. This tendency, called homophily, means that weak ties bridging diverse groups tend to decay at a fast rate because they involve infrequent personal contact with dissimilar people (Burt 2002). This rate of decay was evident in AWARE's declining membership over the years. In 1996, AWARE had around 700 members in total (Rodan 1996). By 2007, this had dwindled to around 200 members. Of this, only 20 to 40 members attended the annual general meetings prior to 2009 (Hussain 2009; Dana Lam-Teo and Margaret Thomas, pers. comm.). Table 1 below shows how the number of new active members in AWARE grew significantly from 2007–8 compared to the years before.

Table 1 New Active Members in AWARE (2002–9)

Year Joined	2002	2003	2004	2005	2006	2007	2008	2009
Number of new active members	2	2	3	7	2	14	45	2,965

Source: AWARE data.

As these weak ties decayed, AWARE's social capital was considerably reduced and it became vulnerable to takeover by other, more cohesive, groups. The new guard led by Thio was able to exploit the holes in AWARE's network because it was a group that could act and mobilise quickly as a result of its homogenous membership. At the Anglican Church of Our Saviour, Thio had "mentored" some of the women in the new guard who worshipped in the same church (Hussain 2009). These women shared similar concerns with Thio and joined as active members in 2008 in order to reform AWARE. Josie Lau, for instance, was a member of the same church and had reportedly been involved in a controversial charity drive by the Development Bank of Singapore (DBS) for Focus on the Family, a Christian organisation that views homosexuality as "immoral and contrary to God's plan for the human family" (Dobson 1998; Wong 2009b). With this highly cohesive group around her, Thio was able to portray AWARE as a battleground of family values against immorality. According to Thio, the family unit was under threat by AWARE's alleged acceptance of homosexuality, especially in its sexual education programme.

Thus the irony was that the source of AWARE's strengths, its network structure linking diverse groups together, had become its Achilles heel. The old guard's ties across the organisational network had decayed to the extent that they were no longer attracting many members into the organisation. As a result of the openings this decay created, the hierarchical network of strong ties centered around Thio could mobilise sufficient social capital, through the enforceable trust that they had towards their "feminist mentor", and take over the AWARE executive committee. For example, Josie Lau, once again through the church, was also an acquaintance of the husband of former AWARE president Claire Nazar and was persuaded by Claire to join AWARE at the beginning of 2009. Claire Nazar, in turn, was connected to the old guard of AWARE through her acquaintance with Constance Singam, who invited her to join the Exco in 2008 (Goh 2009). In the aftermath of the takeover, Constance Singam subsequently quit as AWARE advisor as she had been ignored and excluded from meetings (Wong 2009c). From this turn of events, we can see that AWARE's diversity and inclusiveness led it to include members who did not share these values.

Conclusion

The key lesson from the takeover episode is the importance of maintaining ties to the diverse network of groups that AWARE reaches out to. This is to prevent gaps from forming that could be bridged by homogenous groups bound by strong inter-personal ties such as Thio's. The power of network bridges between different groups was demonstrated by the number of people who joined AWARE in order to participate at the 2009 Extraordinary General Meeting (Table 1). In this case, it was not the old guard but the local press and its frequent coverage of the takeover that reached out to other social groups. Many of the new members were more interested in the Secularism versus Religion debate in civil society than in gender issues, but AWARE should maintain ties with them.

AWARE can achieve this by enabling the *reciprocal* flow of information. For instance, AWARE's membership database is basic at best. Their membership forms did not require information like ethnicity and many other fields were optional. The reason was because AWARE wanted to stay true to its value of gender equality and did not wish to categorise women. This, however, meant that AWARE had significant difficulty in identifying and touching base with members beyond its core. Moreover, besides the membership fee, AWARE leaders did not view their membership roll as a resource pool. As Dana Lam-Teo explained, AWARE is "not a members club" (Dana Lam-Teo, pers. comm.). Indeed, AWARE should be open to all women. So why not allow women to become registered members for free, but give paid members voting rights? In this way, AWARE can better reach out to women from diverse social groups, while remaining focused on its core research and policy work.

AWARE's inclusive organisational structure promotes a culture of *constructive* conflict. Conflict can prevent abuses of power, as evidenced when news broke out of the new guard's unilateral spending in excess of AWARE's annual budget. Constructive conflict was evident at the EGM, to the distaste of some participants who preferred more orderly proceedings. But seeking a deliberative consensus is almost always an emotive affair, and the most probable outcome would be a negotiated compromise that unites a large spectrum of people from diverse backgrounds. In a pluralist society like Singapore, the alternative would either be for the strongest party to dominate opposing groups or implement a form of "agonistic pluralism", where conflicting groups exclude one another and each do their own thing (Mouffe 1999). Either way, this would go against the harmony out of diversity that is the bedrock of Singapore (Lee 2009).

Notes

1. I would like to thank Rina Marie and the other AWARE volunteers for providing some of the data used in this chapter.
2. This data was taken from Rodan (1996). The principle of homophily together with AWARE's organisational structure and objectives suggest that the occupational distribution is still representative.

References

Basu, Radha, 2009, "Long-time Member and New Exco Lock Horns", *The Straits Times*, 24 April.

Boon, Darren, 2009, "AWARE Veterans Set The Record Straight", *The Online Citizen*, <http://theonlinecitizen.com/2009/04/aware-veterans-set-the-record-straight/> [accessed 24 Aug. 2009].

Bourdieu, Pierre, 1986, "The Forms of Capital", in *Handbook of Theory and Research for the Sociology of Education*, ed. John G. Richardson. New York: Greenwood Press, pp. 241–58.

Burt, Ronald, 2002, "Bridge Decay", *Social Networks* 24, 4: 333–63.

Diani, Mario, 2003, "Networks and Social Movements: A Research Programme", in *Social Movements and Networks: Relational Approaches to Collective Action*, ed. Mario Diani and Doug McAdam. Oxford: Oxford University Press, pp. 299–319.

Dobson, James, 1998, "The Christian Response to the Homosexual Agenda", *Focus on the Family*, <http://www2.focusonthefamily.com/docstudy/newsletters/A000000804.cfm> [accessed 24 Aug. 2009].

Girard, Monique and Stark, David, 2003, "Heterarchies of Value in Manhattan-Based New Media Firms", *Theory, Culture & Society* 20, 3: 77–105.

Goh, Serene, 2009, "Claire Nazar: Why I Quit As AWARE President", *The Straits Times*, 19 April.

Granovetter, Mark, 1973, "The Strength of Weak Ties", *American Journal of Sociology* 78, 6: 1360–80.

Hussain, Zakir, 2009, "Lawyer's Key Role in AWARE Coup", *The Straits Times*, 24 April.

Lam-Teo, Dana, 2007, "Feminists of All Persuasions", in *Small Steps, Giant Leaps: A History of AWARE and the Women's Movement in Singapore*, ed. Mandakini Arora. Singapore: AWARE, pp. 169–73.

Lee Hsien Loong, 2009, "National Day Rally", *asiaOne News*, <http://www.asiaone.com/specials/nationalrally_09/> [accessed 24 Aug. 2009].

Low, Aaron and Au Yong, Jeremy, 2009, "Civil Society and Leadership Fights", *The Straits Times*, 18 April.

Lyons, Lenore, 2007, "The Birth of AWARE", in *Small Steps, Giant Leaps: A History of AWARE and the Women's Movement in Singapore*, ed. Mandakini Arora. Singapore: AWARE, pp. 84–117.

Mouffe, Chantal, 1999, "Deliberative Democracy or Agonistic Pluralism?" *Social Research* 66, 3: 745–58.

Portes, Alejandro, 1998, "Social Capital: Its Origins and Applications in Modern Sociology", *Annual Review of Sociology* 24: 1–24.

Powell, Walter W., 1990, "Neither Market Nor Hierarchy: Network Forms of Organization", *Research in Organizational Behavior* 12: 295–336.

Rodan, Garry, 1996, "State-Society Relations and Political Opposition in Singapore", in *Political Oppositions in Industrialising Asia*, ed. Garry Rodan. London: Routledge, pp. 95–127.

Rucht, Dieter, 1996, "The Impact of National Contexts on Social Movement Structures: A Cross-Movement and Cross-National Comparison", in *Comparative Perspectives on Social Movements: Political Opportunities, Mobilizing Structures, and Cultural Framings*, ed. Doug McAdam, John D. McCarthy and Mayer N. Zald. Cambridge: Cambridge University Press, pp. 185–204.

Saw Swee-Hock, 2005, *Population Policies and Programmes in Singapore*. Singapore: Institute of Southeast Asian Studies.

Schmitt, Carl, 2007, *The Concept of the Political*. Chicago: University of Chicago Press.

Simmel, Georg, 1955, *Conflict and the Web of Group Affiliations*. New York: Free Press.

Singam, Constance, 2007, "Women's Activism and Feminism", in *Small Steps, Giant Leaps: A History of AWARE and the Women's Movement in Singapore*, ed. Mandakini Arora. Singapore: AWARE, pp. 14–25.

Tan Dawn Wei, 2009a, "Some Attend The Same Church", *The Straits Times*, 18 April.

———, 2009b, "Locks at AWARE Offices Changed", *The Straits Times*, 24 April.

The Straits Times, 2009a, "Why The Need To Muscle Your Way Into The Executive Committee", 18 April.

———, 2009b, "Group's Agenda 'Took Gay Turn'", 24 April.

Wong Kim Hoh, 2009a, "Unknowns Knock Out Veterans at AWARE Poll", *The Straits Times*, 10 April.

———, 2009b, "DBS Tells Why It Rebuked Josie Lau", *The Straits Times*, 19 April.

———, 2009c, "Constance Singam Quits as AWARE Advisor", *The Straits Times*, 19 April.

CHAPTER 8

Contesting Feminisms: The AWARE Saga

Theresa W. Devasahayam

Introduction

When the AWARE (Association of Women for Action and Research) saga broke out in April 2009, the opportunity to explore local forms of feminism was lost primarily because the issues that loomed large in the media were homosexuality and religion. The tussle between the "old guard", painted as "liberals", and the "new guard", painted as the "Christian Right", also stole analytical attention away from how different interpretations of feminism were expressed in Singapore. Instead in the saga, arguments often took place in silos where issues of sexuality rarely, if ever, overlapped with those of gender equality. To this end, debates over the right to one's own sexuality and sexual orientation were cleanly cleaved from the debates over gender equality in the workplace or social injustice faced by women.

This chapter argues that the debate on sexuality is as much part of the feminist discourse as is ensuring equal rights between men and women. As put forth by Abbott, Wallace and Tyler (2005: 198): "sexuality has been one of the main concerns of feminist theory ... because feminists regard men's control of women's sexuality as one of the key mechanisms through which patriarchy is maintained". Feminists have long been concerned with how women's bodies have become the site of control by men through religion, the state, the media and medical practices (Dyer 1982; Bordo 1993). Feminist theorist bell hooks (2000: 154) encourages women to think inclusively when she says: "all women need to know that they can be politically committed to feminism regardless of their sexual preference". What she sees as a "necessary condition" in the fight for gender equality is sexual freedom: the scope of women to "envision new sexual paradigms" so as to reclaim their own bodies (bell hooks 2000: 150). From this perspective, sexual diversity is an intrinsic part of feminism.

Beyond sexuality, feminist scholars, however, have been consumed with other areas of women's lives marked by gender inequality. Intrinsic to liberal/reformist feminism is the emancipation from unnecessary social, political, or legal restrictions and the creation of a just society in which power and reward are distributed solely on the basis of ability and effort rather than gender identity. For this group of feminists, gender equality can be produced by transforming the division of labour through the repatterning of key institutions — law, work, family, education and media (Bem 1993; Friedan 1963; Lorber 1994; Pateman 1999; Rhode 1997; Schaeffer 2001). Others such as radical feminists have been concerned with women's rights, while recognising that the systems of oppression prevalent in society's most basic structures range from sexuality, class, caste, race and ethnicity to age, although asserting gender as the key feature of social stratification. Questioning the notion of woman as a homogenous category is at the core of black/postcolonial feminism: the assertion among these feminists has been on pinning down the experiences of particular groups of women within the larger subgroup of women based on ethnic difference, racialisation, colonialism and racism (Collins 2001).

Flying in the face of previous schools of feminism that were preoccupied with equality, there have been feminists propagating what has been called difference feminism. The basic assertion among this group of feminists is that men and women are different — biologically, emotionally, psychologically and spiritually. These feminists have made arguments about women's distinctive characteristics for ethical judgment (Day 2000; Friedman 1993; Gilligan 1982; Held 1993); the way women respond to caring behaviours based on their consciousness (Fischer 1995; Reiger 1999; Ruddick 1980); a female-style of communication (Bate and Taylor 1988; Crawford 1995; Tannen 1990, 1993, 1994); an inclination for women to be more emotionally open in their experiences than men (Beutel and Marini 1995; Mirowsky and Ross 1995); women's unique fantasies concerning sexuality and intimacy (Radway 1984; Snitow, Stansell and Thompson 1983); and women's capacity to promote peaceful living conditions with others and their lower levels of aggressive behaviour (A. Campbell 1993; Forcey 2001; Ruddick 1994; Wilson and Musick 1997). While this group of feminists are concerned with a just society, for them "women's ways of being and knowing [are] a healthier template for producing a just society than are the traditional preferences of an androcentric culture [expressed by] male ways of knowing and being" (Lengermann and Niebrugge-Brantley 2003: 444).

In the case of the tussle between the new guard and the old guard, clearly there was an ideological conflict between the old guard propounding inclusiveness and diversity, extending to individuals of different economic backgrounds and sexual orientations, and the new guard focusing on preserving heterosexuality as the normative while asserting for the preservation of the family. The following discussion recounts the tensions between the two camps. The argument put forth here is that while there was a great deal of media attention placed on sexuality, it was the interpretation of feminism that was at the heart of the conflict between the two camps: the old guard pushing for an interpretation of feminism premised on difference and diversity, an inclusive interpretation widely accepted in international feminist circles, while the new guard advancing a more exclusive interpretation that privileged conservative notions of the family and heterosexuality while at the same time acknowledging differences between men and women.

"Being Inclusive": What Is It About?

The old guard has always prided itself in being inclusive, receiving members from all walks of life and backgrounds as it unwaveringly declares itself to be the first feminist organisation in Singapore (Lim 2007). AWARE emerged in the 1980s at a time when there was outrage over government efforts to prop up falling birth rates by encouraging marriage (Lyons 2007). Congregating at the forum "Women's Choices, Women's Lives" held in 1984, the women instrumental in starting up the organisation were firm on one issue: "they were passionate about women's right to choose their own destinies" (Lyons 2007: 87). These women were also opposed to government policies suggesting that women's place was in the home and that their primary role was that of wife and mother. Instead they affirmed that women had "diverse aspirations — some wanted to pursue professional careers, while others wanted to stay home and look after their families; some women wanted to marry, and some wanted children" (Lyons 2007: 88).

AWARE throughout its history has attracted businesswomen and professionals, women in sales and clerical positions, women factory workers, homemakers and students. Some were married with children; others were grandmothers and yet others great-grandmothers. Concerned about how the organisation would be received by the public because of the potential negative connotations attached to feminism, Lena Lim was chosen as the first president — "a woman who embodied the politically acceptable combination of a wife, mother and career woman" (Lyons 2007: 91) — a move thought to be politically correct at that time. Moreover, AWARE's membership included men as well who joined as "Friends of AWARE" right from the start.

It is in this spirit of inclusion that AWARE receives any woman irrespective of sexual orientation. It has been argued that the leadership has been able to accommodate differences "through an insistence on ambivalence ... as a means of negotiating the beliefs and sentiments of individual members.... This means providing room for all women to pursue their own visions of feminism (or women's rights)" (Lyons 2004: 133). In light of this, founding member Dr Kanwaljit Soin's response in the saga did not come as a surprise: "AWARE's founding principle has been inclusiveness and because it has been inclusive we cannot condemn, deny or exclude any woman because of her sexual orientation or because she's been abused by her husband or because she's a single mother" (*The Straits Times* 25 April 2009). Thus, it assumed women were autonomous individuals in their struggle for gender equality and had the right to make choices of their own to effect changes in their lives. Further to this point, that the old guard was not insistent on any one form of sexual orientation among its members provides a strong affirmation of its position on feminism and that "the goal of [the] feminist movement is not to establish codes for a 'politically correct' sexuality" (bell hooks 2000: 154).

As an organisation with diversity at its core, AWARE does not discriminate against any group of women. Instead its mantra of inclusiveness compels it to embrace members who hold to different interpretations of feminism, whether "conservative" or "liberal". The position it adopted is also evidenced in its approach to how it sought to address women's concerns, a point echoed by executive committee (exco) member Margaret Thomas: "If a gay woman comes and asks us for help because she is, say, facing discrimination at work, we will do our best to help her in the same way that we will do our best to help a woman who is being abused by her husband or a pregnant woman who has been sacked because of her pregnancy" (personal communication, 2009). In light of this statement, it is clear that it is not the sexual orientation of the individual that is of paramount importance to how the organisation conducts its activities but rather that the individual who has approached them is a woman. The important factor to AWARE is that all women are unified on the basis of one feature: their identity of being female because of their bodies (Lyons 2004); how they wished to express their sexuality was important to their identity as women to the extent that none were discriminated based on the kind of sexual orientation they upheld. Thus instead of what divided women, the old guard was more concerned about addressing the problems faced by women as a collective. But there was a rationale for the stance they adopted. As suggested by Lyons (2004: 146): "If AWARE members care enough about women's status to want to bring about change, to achieve equality, then the differences become minor."

Till Sexuality Do Us Part

While the old guard was clearly committed to an interpretation of feminism that celebrated diversity, the new guard had interpreted the former's position on sexuality as "liberal". As a label, "liberal" values were subsequently depicted by the new guard as threatening to the conservative values of society, and served as a useful motivation for the April takeover. For the new guard, a string of events in the past had led them to claim that "the women's group had lost sight of its original purpose and had become pro-lesbian and pro-homosexual" (*The Sunday Times* 26 April 2009; *see also The Straits Times* 2 May 2009). The new guard's construction of AWARE's "original purpose" is based on conservative assumptions of what feminism should and should not include. Their assertion was that feminism should not include sexual diversity.

In 2007, the distributors of Spider Lilies, a Taiwanese movie with a lesbian theme, offered to screen it as a charity premiere for AWARE and donated the proceeds to the organisation. The new guard felt that the movie was not appropriate because of its controversial content on sexuality. According to Dr Thio Su Mien, "Another factor which contributed to the view that the old guard was liberal was the male gender awareness workshop organized by AWARE for men. It was conducted by Finnish expatriate Bert Bjarland, an advocate of profeminism, part of the gay movement; this activity was ultra vires the AWARE constitution, and hence unlawful" (pers. comm., 2009).

The Constitution, however, specifically provides for AWARE to educate the public on issues related to gender and to equip "women and men to deal with various forms of discrimination...." It must be noted that AWARE has had male associate members from the start and many of its activities are open to men; as such, the conclusion drawn by the new guard that the old guard's activities targeted at men are unlawful is mistaken. Another criticism the new guard leveled at the old guard was the organisation of a Mother's Day event where mothers and lesbian daughters came together to talk about their experiences. Themes were selected based on what the old guard thought were current issues in the lives of Singaporean women, and in that context the topic of mothers' experiences with lesbian daughters came up one year (Margaret Thomas, pers. comm., 2009).

However, the most publicised point of contention raised in the saga was the Comprehensive Sexuality Education (CSE) programme. Established in 2007, the programme was offered to schools and it was up to the teachers and principals to decide which students would attend the programme. At any one time, the workshops saw 8 to 30 students from ages 12 to 18. Students had the choice of opting out of the programme at any time, if they wished, or if their parents decided that they should. The content of the programme covered a range of topics related to sexuality: HIV/AIDS and STIs (sexually-transmitted infections), teenage pregnancy, negotiating sex, risky sexual behaviour, condom use, and so forth. But what irked the new guard was that, in AWARE's manual guide for its trainers, they felt that homosexuality was treated as a "neutral" word rather than imbued with a negative moral connotation (*The Straits Times* 2 May 2009). Furthermore, the new guard concluded that the AWARE trainer's manual treated anal sex as a neutral term: "anal sex can be healthy or neutral if practised with consent and with a condom" (*The Straits Times* 10 May 2009). Members of the new guard were distressed that the CSE programme had the potential of creating "an entire generation of lesbians", if the young were taught that homosexuality is neutral and normal (*The Straits Times* 24 April 2009). For this reason, they drew the conclusion that the programme was problematic because it potentially threatened to redefine marriage and the family based on the model of the heterosexual family unit.

But on closer scrutiny of the CSE programme, the old guard leadership was committed to the feminist cause through the strategy of knowledge empowerment. Because the programme was established in response to the increasing incidence of teen pregnancy (*The Straits Times* 2 May 2009; *The Straits Times* 22 May 2009), the objective was to empower young girls to protect themselves not only from unwanted pregnancies but also from disease and emotional trauma. The programme was executed by ten trainers "selected for their maturity, open-mindedness and ability to manage young people" (*TODAY* 1 May 2009). In the interactive sessions, trainers did not adopt any one approach. Instead while they emphasised abstinence and "how to say no to sex", at the same time, they also took what might seem to be a "liberal" approach "knowing that kids do not listen, and if they do find themselves in a situation where they are confronted with making the decision to have sex, at least they have the information on how not to get pregnant" (Margaret Thomas, pers. comm., 2009). Cognizant that they had to tread carefully in putting together the materials for this programme because of its sensitive content, AWARE was, over the course of a year, in consultation with a consortium of experts ranging from leading international academics and health professionals working with the International Women's Health Coalition, as well as parents, students and youth social workers and teachers (Dana Lam and Margaret Thomas, pers. comm., 2009; *see also The Straits Times* 9 May 2009). In addition, the materials were put through a rigorous process of internal and external auditing and pilot testing. Thus, it is no surprise that AWARE president Dana Lam reiterated to reporters in the aftermath of the saga that: "the association is not making any apologies for their programmes" (*The New Paper* 2 June 2009).

"Pro-Women, Pro-Family and Pro-Singapore": What Did the "Feminism" of the New Guard Portend?

The fact that a new guard, which had only recently joined the organisation, took over a women's rights NGO posed two immediate questions: were they feminists themselves and, if so, what brand of feminism did they adhere to? There is little doubt that the new guard saw themselves as "feminists" given the emergence of Thio as the self-professed "feminist mentor" to the new exco. To this question, the new guard openly declared to be "pro-women, pro-family and pro-Singapore" (*The Straits Times* 18 April 2009). From this public statement, it was clear how the new guard defined "feminism". In a press release on 15 April 2009, the new guard stated that they intended to "build on the solid foundations laid by the founders of Aware [sic] and will continue to promote the participation of women, on equal terms with men, in the political, social, economic and cultural life of our society. The goal remains to bring about full equality of the sexes and to end all discrimination against women."[1] It had a two-pronged approach. The first was "to empower women to be leaders in our society, in politics, business, the professions and in all areas of endeavour which will benefit our nation". The second was to provide practical help to "working women who are at crossroads about marriage, family and career, and for some the care of aged parents" (Dr Thio Su Mien, pers. comm., 2009).

The new guard neither saw sexual orientation as a legitimate area in which to champion equality nor believed that a woman should have full autonomy over her body when it came to issues like abortion. Furthermore, the new guard had little to offer by way of ethnic or religious diversity given that the takeover was conducted exclusively by Chinese, middle class, Christian women.

Hence, the new guard's concern for gender equality was confined only to political or economic equality in the public domain. It was an interpretation of feminism that fitted their lifestyle and values, and one that excluded those they did not relate to such as homosexuality and lesbianism. While some may argue that this emphasis on gender equality in the public domain derives from the social status of the new guard, all of whom were well educated and professionally respected women, it should be noted that the members of the old guard are also well educated, professionally respected women.

But what was distinctive of the new guard was the simultaneous dismissal of women's sexual diversity and the valorisation of the heterosexually constituted family. The views of the new guard member who became AWARE President during the takeover, Josie Lau, were revealed in the following statements she gave to the press. While recognising that lesbians and homosexuals should be "treated with dignity and respect", she says that "I don't endorse their lifestyle" (*The Straits Times* 3 May 2009). On the organisation's stand on homosexuality, she asserted that it was not the "objective of AWARE to champion the homosexualism [sic] agenda …." (*The Sunday Times* 26 April 2009), but instead it should focus its energies on looking after the affairs of all women rather than prioritising a segment of the female (or for that matter male) populace. It is noteworthy that the old guard's refusal to discriminate against homosexuals was interpreted by the new guard as a prioritisation of a segment of the female population.

The question arises as to whether the new guard's views on the family were derived from feminism or from religious doctrines. According to *The Straits Times* (18 April 2009), 6 of the 11 new guard members on the AWARE executive committee, during the time they were in office, attended the Church of Our Saviour, which has publicly stated its position on women's role and status in the family as subordinated to that of their husbands. Although unanimously the new guard have denied a "church connection" and although they have voiced a concern for gender equality "in politics, business, the professions", their fervour in upholding the conservative ideal of the family, connected to the Christian Right movement in the US, was explicit. And because they were members of a particular church group, this might have meant that they were adamant about promoting lifestyles and values ordained by what they thought would be part of "God's plan". In conjunction with this, they would invariably define marriage as "a sacred union" entered into only by a man and woman. For them, the only morally acceptable form of sexual relations is intercourse between a married couple for purposes of reproduction. Concomitantly, it follows then that the new guard would be opposed on religious grounds to what they defined as feminist-supported ideas of including those with different sexual orientations into the fold.

Moreover, the new guard would not only oppose gay and lesbian rights but also those who are "pro-choice" in relation to abortion, although this issue did not emerge as a conspicuous part of the main debate in the saga. It cannot be denied that the abortion issue is at the heart of feminism because it assumes the protection of the right of the woman to exercise her free will. In as much as feminism aims to preserve a woman's claim to her own body, including her reproductive capacity, a woman has the freedom to express her sexuality in whatever way she wishes, this being integral to the feminist cause of dislodging patriarchy and the power relations between men and women. Particularly on the issue of abortion, the position of the Christian Right stands in opposition to the position of feminists since the former proposes taking away a woman's right to decide on matters concerning her own body.

In spite of the position the new guard had taken on sexuality, it would be difficult to dismiss them entirely as being non-feminist or even anti-feminist. Rather, as this chapter asserts, the new guard was "feminist" to the extent of recognising the need to work towards gender equality in some defined areas. In other areas, however, they were concerned with preserving differences between men and women and notions of "traditional" and "homogeneity" as embodied in the family context. To this extent, they recognised gender differences and, in this regard, may be said to adhere to difference feminism.

Conclusion

Sexual relations are governed by formal and informal social rules concerning whom one may have sexual relations with and how these relationships should be conducted. What requires more analytical attention is how those "rules" are being constructed and debated, by whom, for whom, and why. In some societies, homosexuality is considered tabooed behaviour and, therefore, stigmatised. Some countries like Singapore continue to debate on gay and lesbian sexualities. Although Parliament has debated on repealing Section 377A — the legislation which criminalises homosexuality — this law has since remained.

AWARE has long been committed to egalitarianism and equality irrespective of differences in sexuality long before. It has always fought for an "inclusive feminism", and "consequently, it has [had the potential of] arous[ing] the hostility of powerful vested interests that see feminism as a threat to age-old traditions, structures and patterns of everyday life", as demonstrated in the AWARE saga (Singam 2007: 16).

Such hostility has been expressed in the April 2009 saga over the admission of homosexuality into "inclusive feminism". This prompted the President of AWARE, Dana Lam, to assure the public: "We would like to point out that homosexuality has never been 'a major issue' for the Association of Women for Action and Research (Aware). Our stand, throughout the 24 years of our existence, has been identical to that of the Government.... The allegation of a 'gay agenda' was made by Dr Thio Su Mien, and the team of women she handpicked to join Aware and take over its leadership, on the strengths of bits of information taken out of context and strung together to create an imaginary and inaccurate picture of Aware's [sic] activities" (*The Straits Times* 16 May 2009).

In a nutshell, the entire saga arose out of the Christian Right's attempt to delink issues of gender equality and sexual freedoms, including individual choices in expressing one's sexuality irrespective of orientation. Furthermore, AWARE as an organisation certainly should not be perceived as anti-heterosexual since the majority of its members are engaged in heterosexual relationships. Thus, the old guard was fully aware of the need to accommodate diverse forms of sexuality given its stance as a secular and diverse NGO, and it was this broad acceptance and climate of respect that they saw to be useful as a powerful force of resistance against patriarchal values. Hence, suspicions of the new guard came up particularly because of their religious affiliation, which motivated their stated opposition to the inclusion of homosexuality as a valid form of sexual expression, thereby threatening the spirit of diversity and respect nurtured by the organisation.

The central question of reclaiming the (female) body and the notion of asserting one's control over one's body was a focal point of contention in the entire saga, reflecting how feminism has evolved in Singapore. The AWARE saga demonstrated that in multi-cultural Singapore, the acceptance of alternative sexualities and life-choices cannot be assumed but is part of a feminism that has to assert its right to be inclusive and diverse in the face of hostile interests. It is to this extent that feminism was very much alive in the AWARE saga, as the feminist debates on sexuality were framed in all the events constituting the entire episode.

Note

1. "A copy of this press statement was released to the press on the night of 15 April 2009 after Josie Lau who had just been appointed president at an emergency Exco meeting spoke to the press" (Dr. Thio Su Mien, pers. comm., 2009); see also *The Straits Times* Forum letter dated 2 June 2009 entitled "'New exco' didn't stonewall reporters" by Jenica Chua who was the then Hon. Secretary, paragraphs 4 and 5 which referred to this press statement.

References

Abbott, Pamela, Wallace, Claire and Melissa Tyler, 2005, *An Introduction to Sociology: Feminist Perspectives*, 3rd Edition. London: Routledge.

Bate, Barbara and Anita Taylor, 1988, *Women Communicating: Studies of Women's Talk*. Norwood, New Jersey: Ablex.

bell hooks, 2000, *Feminist Theory: From Margin to Center*. Cambridge, Massachusetts: South End Press.

Bem, Sandra L.,1993, *The Lenses of Gender: Transforming Debates on Sexual Inequality*. New Haven: Yale University Press.

Beutel, Ann M. and Margaret M. Marini, 1995, "Gender and Values", *American Sociological Review* 60: 436–48.

Bordo, Susan, 1995, *Unbearable Weight: Feminism, Western Culture, and the Body*. Berkeley and Los Angeles, California: University of California Press.

Campbell, Anne, 1993, *Men, Women and Aggression*. New York: Basic Books.

Collins, Patricia H., 2001, "Womanism and Black Feminism", in *Issues in Feminism: An Introduction to Women's Studies*, ed. Sheila Ruth. California: Mayfield Publishing.

Constitution of the Association of Women for Action and Research, 1985 (updated). Singapore: AWARE.

Crawford, Mary, 1995, *Talking Difference: On Gender and Language*. Newbury Park, California: Sage.

Day, Kristen, 2000, "The Ethic of Care and Women's Experiences of Public Space", *Journal of Environmental Psychology* 20: 103–24.

Dyer, Gillian, 1982, *Advertising as Communication*. London: Methuen.

Fischer, Sue, 1995, *Nursing Wounds: Nurse Practitioners, Doctors, Women Patients and the Negotiation of Meaning*. New Brunswick, New Jersey: Rutgers University Press.

Forcey, Linda R., 2001, "Feminist Perspectives on Mothering and Peace", *Journal of the Association for Research on Mothering* 3(2): 155–74.

Friedan, Betty, 1963, *The Feminine Mystique*. New York: Dell.

Friedman, Marilyn, 1993, *What are Friends for? Feminist Perspectives on Personal Relationships and Moral Theory*. Ithaca, New York: Cornell University Press.

Gilligan, Carol, 1982, *In a Different Voice: Psychological Theory and Women's Development*. Cambridge, Massachusetts: Harvard University Press.

Held, Virginia, 1993, *Feminist Morality: Transforming Culture, Society and Politics*. Chicago: University of Chicago Press.

Lengermann, Patricia M. and Jill Niebrugge-Brantley, 2003, "Contemporary Feminist Theory", in *Sociological Theory*, ed. George Ritzer and Douglas J. Goodman. New York: McGraw-Hill.

Lim, Lena, 2007, "Challenges Ahead", in *Small Steps, Giant Leaps: A History of AWARE and the Women's Movement in Singapore*, ed. Mandakini Arora. Singapore: The Association of Women for Action and Research.

Lorber, Judith, 1994, *Paradoxes of Gender*. New Haven: Yale University Press.

Lyons, Lenore, 2004, *A State of Ambivalence: The Feminist Movement in Singapore*. Leiden: Brill.

————, 2007, "The Birth of AWARE", in *Small Steps, Giant Leaps: A History of AWARE and the Women's Movement in Singapore*, ed. Mandakini Arora. Singapore: The Association of Women for Action and Research.

Mirowsky, John and Catherine Ross, 1995, "Sex Differences in Distress: Real or Artifact?" *American Sociological Review* 60: 449–68.

Pateman, Carole, 1999, "Beyond the Sexual Contract?" in *Rewriting the Sexual Contract*, ed. Geoff Dench. New Brunswick, New Jersey: Transaction.

Radway, Janice, 1984, *Reading the Romance: Women, Patriarchy and Popular Culture*. Chapel Hill: University of North Carolina Press.

Reiger, Karreen, 1999, "'Sort of Part of the Women's Movement. But Different': Mothers' Organisations and Australian Feminism", *Women's Studies International Forum* 22(6): 585–95.

Rhode, Deborah L., 1997, *Speaking of Sex: The Denial of Gender Inequality*. Cambridge, Massachusetts: Harvard University Press.

Ruddick, Sara, 1980, "Maternal Thinking", *Feminist Studies* 6: 342–67.

_____, 1994, "Notes towards a Feminist Maternal Peace Politics", in *Living with Contradictions: Controversies in Feminist Social Ethics*, ed. Alison M. Jagger. Boulder, Colorado: Westview Press.

Schaeffer, Denise, 2001, "Feminism and Liberalism Reconsidered: The Case of Catherine MacKinnon", *American Political Science Review* 95: 699–708.

Singam, Constance, 2007, "Women's Activism and Feminism", in *Small Steps, Giant Leaps: A History of AWARE and the Women's Movement in Singapore*, ed. Mandakini Arora. Singapore: The Association of Women for Action and Research.

Snitow, Ann B., Stansell, Christine and Sharon Thompson, 1983, *Powers of Desires: The Politics of Sexuality*. New York: Monthly Review Press.

Tannen, Deborah, 1990, *You Just Don't Understand: Women and Men in Conversation*. New York: William Morrow.

_____, 1994, *Gender and Discourse*. New York: Oxford.

Tannen, Deborah (ed.), 1993, *Gender and Conversational Interaction*. New York: Oxford.

The New Paper, 2 June 2009, "We're sorry for 'trauma' but not for our programmes".

The Straits Times, 18 April 2009, "The Saga Thus Far ....".

_____, 24 April 2009, "Dr Thio upset about sexuality programme", by Zakir Hussain.

_____, 25 April 2009, "Too diversified or too focused? Which is it?" by Wong Kim Hoh.

_____, 2 May 2009, "How it Got to This", by Wong Kim Hoh.

_____, 3 May 2009, "Josie Lau's 3 weeks in the hot seat", by Sumiko Tan.

_____, 9 May 2009, "Suspension of Aware Programme Sends Wrong Message", Forum Page by Alexandra Serrenti.

_____, 10 May 2009, "Sexuality 101", by Shuli Sudderuddin.

_____, 16 May 2009, "Aware has never had a 'gay agenda'", Forum Page by Dana Lam.

_____, 22 May 2009, "MOE tightens vetting of Sexuality Education", by Theresa Tan.

————, 2 June 2009, "'New exco' didn't stonewall reporters", Forum Page by Jenica Chua.

The Sunday Times, 26 April 2009, "Nothing 'sneaky' about elections".

TODAY, 1 May 2009, "Guided or Misguided?" by Alicia Wong and Lin Yanqin.

Wilson, John and Mark Musick, 1997, "Who Cares? Towards an Integrated Theory of Volunteer Work", *American Sociological Review* 60: 694–713.

CHAPTER 9

Shut Up and Sit Down! Stand Up and Speak Out!: The AWARE EGM as Performance of Civil Society in Singapore

Lai Ah Eng[1]

Prelude to the Performance

Some sense of the build-up and behind-the-scene developments leading to the EGM is necessary to understanding its actual performance and significance. Suffice here to summarise that at the 24th Association of Women for Action and Research (AWARE) Annual General Meeting (AGM) held on 28 March 2009, 9 positions out of a total of 12 of the association's executive committee (Exco) went to new members, and that a spike in membership from a low of 253 in 2008 to about 400 had been noticed in the weeks leading up to the AGM. According to two life members whose suspicions were aroused at the meeting (which I did not attend), it was suggested to those nominated for the main positions to first participate in an AWARE sub-committee, as these positions entail experience and responsibility. As they did not retract their nominations, they were then asked to clarify their position on feminism and gender equality, since AWARE is an openly declared feminist organisation based on principles of gender equality and inclusiveness. They were also asked their position specifically on homosexuality as there was a strong suspicion that they were anti-gay.[2] Their responses were not forthcoming. They were voted in, together with two other regular volunteers.

In the immediate days following the new guard's election, some alarmed members met to discuss what they suspected was a deliberate takeover and on an appropriate course of action. At one such gathering I attended, it was clarified that an already identified loophole in AWARE's Constitution that had not been plugged through formal regulation in time was what had allowed the instant eligibility to run for office without prior volunteer service in the organisation. It was also pointed out that the majority Exco members seemed to act as a team and excluded the other minority elected members at meetings, was not responsive to questions, were high handed with AWARE staff, changed the AWARE office computer service system immediately and went about selectively acquiring confidential data. It was also revealed, through Internet search and contacts, that at least six of them had connections to the evangelical Church of Our Saviour (COOS) known for its conservative theological position on social issues. But besides that, no one knew who they were as they had never been seen at AWARE events before.

The gathering discussed several points: whether there was indeed a calculated move to take over AWARE's Exco and what might be the new guard's intention; whether its religious background and church stand on homosexuality was a major motivating factor in the move and how this might affect its mission and agenda for AWARE; and whether its behaviour thus far indicated an exclusivist and ill-fitted approach to working with others. Should we be "doves", gracious in defeat, call for a meeting with the new team to get to know them? Or we should be "hawks", always alert and ready to pounce, and call for an extraordinary meeting to cast a vote of no confidence against it? What would be justifiable grounds for calling such a vote — a lack of experience and non-transparent and unreasonable behaviour in AWARE? Could their religious background and stand be confirmed and substantively used against them? Some preferred an ordinary over an extraordinary meeting as being fairer in a "let's see how they respond" and "give them a chance" approach. Those who preferred to "vote them out" argued that the team's behaviour thus far, coupled with their religious background and anti-homosexuality tendencies, indicated a planned conspiracy and portended a long-term danger to AWARE even as their exact motives were not yet fully understood.

We grappled with the pros and cons of both as well as legal implications but no decision was arrived at even as the clock struck midnight.

Meanwhile, events related to AWARE became public news and over the following days, the plot thickened as more events were reported. The picture that was beginning to emerge in full public view grew more coherent each day — that of an orchestrated takeover of AWARE by a group of women from a church with conservative views on sexuality. But why take over AWARE? Why not set up its own organisation? What was their agenda? Then came a jaw-dropping piece of news — that senior lawyer Dr Thio Su Mien, self-described "feminist mentor" had played a key role in bringing about the change of leadership at AWARE as she was disturbed by what she saw as signs of AWARE's promotion of lesbianism and homosexuality.[3] Among those she mentored were Lau, who was also the wife of her nephew. With Thio's public revelation, what some old guard members had suspected was now provided proof and substantiation that came directly from the horse's mouth. Meanwhile, a requisition for an EGM had been started, to pass a resolution that the current Exco had lost the mandate and confidence of AWARE members and should be removed and replaced with a new elected committee. With Thio's revelation, the requisition quickly grew in momentum, and by 14 April the requisition with 160 signatures, which fulfilled the requisite 10 per cent of AWARE membership for the EGM to be called within two weeks, was submitted. The stage was set for a struggle within AWARE.

Both sides recognised that the number of registered voting members eligible was crucial and lost no time in recruiting them. How the new guard rounded up support remains to be better known, but church support was definitely involved.[4] On the old guard's side, founding, life and long time members were contacted and their friends and friends of friends were approached through personal and new media means, such as websites, blogs, Facebook and Twitter. Unsolicited help was also received from those unknown to them before, offering their time and expertise such as on legal issues and new media use, and it was through such offers that free legal advice was obtained and the "we-are-aware.sg" website and hotline 98180516 were set up within two days by volunteers. The old guard's side also found supporters among gay women and those who clearly reacted to what they saw as the conservative anti-gay position of Thio and COOS. There was also considerable support from Singaporeans and others overseas, expressed mostly through blogs.

As the membership drive on both sides heated up, there were more dramatic moments right up to the eve of the EGM. These included changes of venue because of police intervention on grounds of public law and order; the pastor of COOS announcing that his earlier call for his congregation to support Josie and "sisters" was wrong; the President of the National Council of Churches of Singapore (NCCS) clarifying that NCCS did not condone churches getting involved in the AWARE saga or pulpits being used for that purpose; and the Minister of Home Affairs warning against the saga being seen in religious terms.[5] While these final moments before the EGM might have scared off some, they might have drawn others to it.

Both sides recognised the need to prepare well for the EGM battle — as a contest of voting power and as a keenly watched public event. How the new guard prepared remains to be better known, although it is clear from the EGM itself that it had mobilised volunteers. On the old guard's side, I witnessed a flurry of organisation and activity on three day-long occasions. At the first, I joined a general discussion on the main issues to focus on at the EGM, the broad strategies to take, anticipation of the other side's strategies and tactics, and legal issues. At the second, there was some more discussion of main issues, strategies A–D and their possible outcomes. Then we broke up into smaller teams. There was a team of inner-circle members that planned for winning or losing, a second for mobilisation and a third on legal issues. I found myself in a fourth team of "speakers" that broke up into small groups each with the responsibility of raising one key issue and framing questions and comments around it. Re-gathering, all "speakers" and volunteers discussed their issues and tried out framing of questions and comments until close to midnight.

I found the third occasion which took place on the EGM's eve the most amazing. There were many more volunteers. Camaraderie was strong and the belief to do right by AWARE was palpable on every face. The largely expanded mobilisation team had obviously done much work — there were T-shirts, placards and fact sheets all ready for packing. The team leader briefed on mobilisation coverage and it seemed that every aspect, from volunteer recruitment and deployment, administration, logistics, mass communication and seating arrangements to sudden illness and hungry stomachs, had been covered with about 120 volunteers in place, both for the EGM's preparation and for the event itself. We discussed crowd control, how to stay calm and act dignified if provoked, and cheers and chants (the suggestion to shout "shame! shame!" was quickly shot down as "too rude"; someone made his friend promise he and his angry gay friends would not turn up). The "win-or-lose" team briefed on what we would do "if we lost", that is, announce the immediate set up of an alternative organisation and its agenda to members and supporters. The legal team said it was still meeting. The third group of about ten speakers looked the least ready and was the most experimental. It imagined what the EGM would be like ("smooth" and "rough" scenarios), role-played how the chairperson Josie Lau might manage it (her competence and strategy, possible delay tactics) and, most important, how the speakers would take turns to go up to ask key questions and make comments. The first rounds of role playing were pathetic as they hesitated and fumbled with phrasing, cracked up with laughter and did not seem to have any "fire in the belly", so much so that someone said "we are actually going to lose at the rate we go". We certainly did not seem confident. Some had never stood up to speak to a crowd (how large and scary would it be?), and now each was practising hard to get her one point across concisely and with firmness.

Interestingly, I observed that it was strongly believed that the new guard would be highly mobilised in numbers, with supporters un- questioningly obedient on orders (due to church organisation and socialisation), as well as possibly provocative and intimidating in beha- viour (the new guard had brought some husbands to guard the AWARE premises and they were reportedly aggressive to old members and staff). On the old guard's side, it was not sure if the call for supporters to register as voting members would be effective, for, as someone said, "it's hard to organise our side. We are not like the 'Christian fundies', we live and let live. And we have our own minds, we don't just obey. And some of us are rather laid back." Indeed, it was believed that the old guard might be overwhelmed by numbers on the day itself and therefore lose. Even a personal friend, a long time political observer of Singapore politics, had earlier phoned up to say "Your side may look like a rainbow coalition at the press conference. But I think your side will lose at the EGM, you will be outnumbered." In short, the battle was likely to be like David versus Goliath. The plan was that if we were outnumbered, we would go down fighting. It took another dormant founding member who had turned up to ask angrily: "Why do you keep thinking you are going to lose? What's the point of fighting if you think you are going to lose?". "When you fight, you fight to win!" she thundered! We practised some more verbal fighting, in between bouts of feeding ourselves with food and humour about our uncertain state, till we were exhausted. I went home around midnight with these thoughts swimming in my head: Fight, fight, fight! Go down fighting! Fight to win!

The EGM as Performance of Civil Society

As I entered the cavernous convention centre of Suntec City, I immediately thought to myself: How did it come to this? Who would have imagined that on the eve of AWARE's 25th anniversary, we would have to fight to regain control of the organisation? The long queues of people lining up to register as members and to get into the hall, the hired security, the organised supporters of both sides, the atmosphere of anticipation and tension — it was simply surreal. What a contrast to the day 24 years ago in humble Cairnhill Community Centre where the founding team openly announced, to a crowd of about 100 supporters and observers, the setting up of AWARE, what it stood for and its agenda, with each of the founding members taking turns to speak on why she personally chose to join it and what she was responsible for. Now, the hall seemed too huge and the situation too uncertain. But when I saw the familiar faces of life and long time members and the determined looks of volunteers, I felt that spirit of 24 years ago return. And then I knew why, earlier in the day, I had so carefully composed my one point for the big battle.

The new guard appeared prepared for the EGM. Their ushers wore bright red T-shirts that said "PRO-WOMEN, PRO-FAMILY, PRO-SINGAPORE". I noticed they were mostly middle-aged women and men. The system for registration, checking for legitimate membership and right to vote was orderly and systematic and security police were stationed strategically to cope with the huge crowd. The old guard's mobilisation "ushers and roamers" team, mostly young women, were in identifiable white T-shirts with the double meaning "WE ARE AWARE" slogan, and handed out flowers and an information pack of flyers besides ensuring orderly queuing. The cover sheet said: "For All Women — Trust, Respect, and Choice" and carried the message "Make your stand, keep calm and be respectful, whatever the outcome the work will continue". In one flyer titled "How You Can Make a Difference Today", "Fair. Transparent. Dignified." was spelt out as the hope for the EGM, and supporters were urged to practise patience (to last a long and challenging day), trust (in representatives to speak), dignity and respect (*vis-à-vis* supporters from the other side), and emotional well being (stay positive). A second flyer listed in brief "What AWARE Has Done For Me", two others spelt out the grounds for "Why This Extraordinary General Meeting" and "Why It is So Important That the Vote of No Confidence is Carried", and a final one provided background information on AWARE's services, education and research, with a chronology of its achievements over its 24 years of existence. There was also a red "We ARE AWARE" placard provided for waving about if needed. The "white shirts" also consisted of groups of leaders for cheers (and walk-out if need be); seat "warmers" (for securing strategic seats near microphones and aisle for speakers); peacekeepers, calmers and huggers (in case of quarrels, intimidation and provocation); scrutineers (to witness fair membership registration and vote counting); food providers, messengers and first-aiders; and videographers and photographers. It had also prepared a "sanctuary" (space offered by a restaurant nearby for individuals to retreat to for a break and for the old guard to re-gather in case of defeat). It was a strange and unprecedented sight — young "white shirts" versus middle-aged "red shirts", but they kept a respectful distance from each other. In a different situation, they could have been groups of mothers and daughters stretching out to hug each other.

Inside the meeting hall, a stage had been set and seating sections clearly demarcated, with one rear section for non-voting associate members and another front section cordoned off (for whom, I wondered). There were also two front rows of reserved VIP seats (for whom, I wondered again). As people streamed in, I recognised some familiar faces and public figures — university colleagues and students, performing artistes, writers, journalists, other civil society activists, diplomats' wives, a famous cook, and even some former political detainees. The diversities of women were striking —young, middle-aged and old; ethnically mixed; locals (mostly) and expatriates (a few). We sat in small groups for support.

Close to the scheduled start of the meeting at 2 p.m., I received my first mass SMS message from the mobilisation team that said: "We ARE AWARE, Welcome to the EGM. We hope you are comfortable. You will be hearing from us via SMS throughout the day." I noticed that the VIP rows began to be taken by women some of whom I recognised as from Protestant Christian churches (I knew at least three of them personally). Some founding and life AWARE members decided to move to the VIP seats which they considered rightfully theirs.

I could not help thinking that the new guard could have shown some common courtesy and strategic sense of public relations to seek out and introduce themselves to the first AWARE president and founding members and to invite them to the VIP seats. When the meeting finally began half an hour late because of the long queues, the hall was filled to capacity except for the cordoned section in front — my guess was that it was for the expected busloads of new guard supporters but they had either not turned up or did not register in time before the door closed. But even with a bird's eye view, one could not ascertain which side had more supporters. The air was one of intense anticipation and uncertainty, and on the AWARE side, extreme alertness but not anger. Not yet, until the performance began, and it was aroused unexpectedly and early.

The first dramatic moments began within the first five minutes of the meeting. Immediately after the rules for meeting were spelt out, AWARE president Josie Lau asked a male associate member Siew Kum Hong to move from the voters section to the section for associate members. The old guard protested that he was their legal adviser and should sit amongst them. Lau responded with a firm voice of authority: "Can the security step in please." I noticed that a desk had been provided for the new guard's legal counsel and two note-takers but not for the AWARE side. Siew ignored Lau's repeated requests to move and the security did not step in. Lau began her speech with her background as a mother and her joining AWARE because of her interests in women's issues, education and gender equality, but was barely into her third sentence when someone interrupted her with "point of order!" This was inaudible to those sitting at the back and some people called for the microphones to be switched on. Lau called for order. Some people again called "turn on the mikes!" Lau responded authoritatively with "... Unruly behaviour will be escorted out. What are you afraid of? Let me get on with my business ... when it's time to speak, the mikes will be turned on ...." The floor shouted for the microphones. Lau again called on the security to stop unruly behaviour, joined by her Honorary Treasurer Maureen Ong who said: "Security, please escort anybody caught making noise out. Security! Now! Immediately!" Lau reiterated: "I am the President and I preside over the meeting. Sit down! Security, please escort anybody disrupting the meeting out NOW!" More and louder voices shouted for the microphones to be turned on. I could almost feel temperatures rise. I received the first mass SMS message "Keep Calm Be Dignified".

The security seemed uncertain what to do. I thought that invoking the security and having the microphones turned off were bad first moves when facing an unknown or unsympathetic crowd.[6] Even the new guard's legal advisor said, "In terms of strict fairness, the mikes should be left open." But he also asked that Lau be given the opportunity to address the members.

Lau continued with her speech — on the legitimate election of her team and the non-involvement of COOS in their joining AWARE, the history and achievements of AWARE, her plans for the future and the credentials of individual team members. But as she spoke, the new guard's supporters got agitated and murmuring grew. Quite apart from the controversial issue of the election's legitimacy and COOS' involvement, they felt that the new guard was appropriating what others had worked on and contributed to. Even I felt a sense of anger to see some of AWARE's early projects I had worked on with others being listed by this unknown and highly suspect team. Lau's acknowledgement of the work and contributions of founders and members seemed insincere and unconvincing to me. Nor did her team's curriculum vitae details impress — the majority of AWARE members have equally strong credentials — and I felt this was yet another instance of poor judgment when facing well-qualified and highly experienced AWARE women. Then came the first big unexpected turning point. Old guard Margaret Thomas, whose task was to be alert to points of order and rules of speaking in an EGM and on any possible delay tactics, stood up and said: "Sorry, Josie, you have exceeded your three minutes [allotted for speaking]." New guard Assistant Honorary Treasurer Sally Ang snapped angrily: "No disruption! Shut up and sit down!" The old guard's supporters gasped and went wild. Some stood up to shout. With that and despite Lau's apology, the angry and antagonistic tone first raised over the use of security to maintain order and the turning off of microphones was set for the rest of the meeting. I received the second mass SMS message "Keep Calm Be Dignified".

It is impossible here to provide a blow-by-blow account of the next seven hours, but a sequential selection of important or electrifying moments and key turning points — and there were unexpectedly many — offers a sense of how civil society engagement was performed in an unprecedented and dramatic fashion. After Lau's apology for Ang's outburst, she continued with the assurance that AWARE would remain a secular organisation, that gay women seeking help from AWARE would receive support and counselling, that abused women will be protected under the Women's Charter, and that her team invited women of all races to join. She had the chance to complete her speech, but it seemed the audience did not really hear her let alone take her seriously or believe her. Old guard Thomas reminded that this was an EGM, not an AGM, and asked that the requisition for the EGM be dealt with first. Lau agreed, to the surprise of those who thought she might use further delay tactics.

The next part of the meeting was a crucial legal one. A brief exchange took place between both sides' legal counsels as to whether the immediate removal of the current Exco upon a successful vote of no confidence was legally binding and whether a replacement Exco could indeed be appointed at an EGM. The old guard's legal team cited Articles 9 and 12 of the AWARE Constitution: "... If the members today decide that we have no confidence in the Exco, then they should leave." The new guard and its legal counsel differed but agreed that voting could take place. It was announced to all that voting on the motion that "the Current Exco has lost the mandate and confidence of the members of the Society to continue as Exco", would be in three parts: (1) that the Current Exco has not acted and is not acting in the best interest of the Society, (2) does not appreciate or share the values of the Society, and (3) does not have the requisite experience of carrying out the Society's work or is otherwise inadequate to further the Society's objectives.

Once voting procedures were explained and the floor declared open for discussion, the first batch of old guard speakers rushed to line up to speak and took on a non-stop attack on the behaviour of the new guard since it took office. Old guard member Dana Lam: "... since you began, you have dismissed key personnel, you dismissed long serving volunteers ... you have obsessed over the security ... changed locks at night ... you are the wrong fit for our association." Braema Mathi: "... I struggled with your [legal] election ... I struggled to understand what you were going to do because the silence was so overpowering. Then finally, the information came out.... We asked to have a simple discussion on how to run today's meeting, we wrote and phoned for a logistics meeting, civil meeting, but you gave no response. We are chided like children.... It is not valid to have the mikes off. On that note alone, I say you are not the right representative." Constance Singam: "... You have very nicely listed the achievements of AWARE ... where were you when we worked ... where were you when women were abused and battered in their homes? Where were you when women were denied equal medical benefits? WHERE WERE YOU?" Other speakers' tirades: "... for three weeks you have tried to impress us with wanting to improve the status of women. Then on 23 April the reasons were revealed ... you have not been open and honest with us since the beginning ...."; "... your pastor openly used the pulpit to gain support for you and your team. As a non-Christian, I am afraid of your insidious measure to enter a secular organisation. I am now afraid of Christians ...."; "I see all of you are of the same faith, same church, same race. Where is the diversity?" I was struck by the speakers' passion and anger. At role play and practice, they were unconvincing. But this was for real, and they sprang into action, their thoughts flying out sharp and pointed, like arrows. And after each had spoken, the supporters roared while the new guard appealed for right of reply and for order. Honorary treasurer Maureen: "If there's no right of reply, there is no debate. There must be right of reply." Lau: "Can we have a chance to reply? It is only fair. Otherwise, it is undemocratic ...." But the old guard's supporters' roars were loud and incessant. The performance had taken yet another turn in which it was now open for the audience's active participation. And the old guard's supporters responded, not by instruction but in spontaneity, to each charge and allegation against the new guard.

As if the atmosphere was not charged enough, the next unexpected episode happened — Thio Su Mien was invited by Lau to speak. This outraged some old guard supporters who had lined up to speak and they screamed: "Line up! Line up!" The commotion was deafening. I thought to myself: "OK, she didn't queue up. But here was the feminist mentor in person! Why not let her speak and let her be judged?" It was as if others shared the thought and someone gave her the mike. She said: "... Please listen. I believe I am a feminist mentor because ... some of us live our lives to celebrate feminism. I believe because I am a feminist that you have put me in your book. Here, I am on page 73 [waves an AWARE publication and points to a page] ... First female Dean of law school ... I am very charmed that I am in your book...." The old guard's supporters went wild with disbelief. When order was finally restored somewhat, she was allowed to continue: "... Show some respect here, okay? You have said you celebrate women ... have some respect for your elders...." The jeers seemed to hit the roof and bounce back to reverberate through the whole hall. Someone screamed: "Earn the respect!" I received the third mass SMS message "Keep Calm Be Dignified". Order seemed unrestorable and Thio gave up, shaking her head as she said, "well, if the world has come to this, so be it". I thought Thio was definitely out of touch with the world of the there and then — a hall full of angry women — as was Lau, the Chair who had allowed Thio to continue. I also could not help wondering: now where is the emotional intelligence of this mentor? The supporters started to chant "We are AWARE! We are AWARE! We are AWARE!" Placards were waved for the first time.[7]

Voting time was a serious but relatively smooth affair. Everyone was keen to cast their vote. After all, this was the main reason for the event. Some groups in red T-shirts were seen to leave the hall immediately after the voting, without waiting for the final outcome. It was announced that the counting of votes would proceed in a separate Boardroom, to be undertaken by professional scrutineers hired from Deloitte & Touche and witnessed by AWARE scrutineers. The voting period provided a reprieve from the uproarious "Page 73" episode. But it also turned out to be the lull before the storm.

While waiting for the votes to be counted, the new guard proposed to move on to the next item: constitutional amendments. "What constitutional amendments?" one supporter turned around to ask me. I did not know either. I managed to hear only the following amidst the sounds of the gathering storm: "... we have not received your notes to the constitutional amendments. How on earth do you expect us to vote on it now?" (Old guard); "It's available at the door ... we can give you five minute to go through it" (Lau); and "... the complexity of this proposal ... you should seriously consider withholding this so everyone has a chance to read ...," There was an inaudible exchange between both sides and their counsels, and the item was dropped. Next, Lau asked for right of reply to "all the questions and accusations hurled at us" and clarified on the main controversial points: her team members did not know each other even though they were from the same church; the two-week silence was because of the sudden resignation of Claire Nazar; the need for security review of the AWARE centre; the termination and reappointment of sub-committees as a logical process with the change of Exco; the dismissal of the AWARE centre manager for insubordination; and denial of insensitivity to diversity in her committee. No one took her up any further on these matters. Her explanation seemed to have come too late, if at all they could be believed by the old guard's supporters. Instead, someone raised a question on expenditure incurred by the Exco thus far. And the sudden storm started.

"... The current constitution states that the executive committee has power to authorise signature of amount not exceeding $20,000 ... and have you authorised more than $20,000? ... How are you going to pay for this? Personally?" The questioner, who was not a representative speaker, spoke like a lawyer in court. Maureen Ong, honorary treasurer, started to explain the reason for the change of venue from a smaller and cheaper one to a larger one but was interrupted by the questioner: "Madam, I am asking you to account for the amount of money that the committee has spent." Ong explained that the enlarged membership to 3,000 meant that she had to get the Suntec City Hall to accommodate all members but which cost $22,000. At hearing this sum, there was a prolonged uproar from the old guard's supporters. Said the questioner: "I am a practising lawyer and I say you have breached *ultra vires* the constitution by spending over the limit. The maximum you are allowed to spend is $20,000 and anything above; you need to seek the members' approval. You are not above the law." Near pandemonium broke out. One new guard supporter protested: "I thought women are all civilised ... in an AGM, follow the house rules strictly!" Lau called for order and the security to step in to "escort this lady out!" She and Ong took pains to explain the need to shift to a larger venue within a matter of days because of the sudden expansion of membership caused by the old guard (but said nothing about the new guard's recruitment). "How do you shoot a moving target? ... the Exco was very concerned about the EGM ... we had to make sure that the organisation is done in a professional manner ... and that is why we got Board room, scrutineers from Deloitte — one of the big four, and the police ... there were so many things we had to do." The reply came fast: "I appreciate that ... I emailed you four times asking to meet so that we can work out the organisation of the EGM together but you did not respond...." I noticed that a long queue of people from the floor had lined up to speak. The ten representative speakers who had practised were not among them. They came forth from the floor, spontaneously.

The momentum on the money matter continued to build up. Someone from the floor: "I own a PR agency. We also organise events ... I am surprised you have to spend all this money to organise this event ... when we work in a civil society organisation, we try not to spend money ... paying event organiser, scrutineers, this should never happen. What you should do is to ask around for help, ask somebody to offer a free stage ...." Another member from the floor: "I have been a professional fundraiser ... I am saddened to hear of the amount spent on this event that could have been put to better use ... I know how much it costs to employ lawyers, events agency ... please give me a figure. $50,000? $100,000? How much have you spent in the one month as Exco?" Ong gave an estimate of $90,000 and the AWARE supporters let out howls of outrage. The queue grew longer. Comments flew fast and furious: "This is absolutely horrifying. You have spent $70,000 above the accepted limit!" "I understand that a legal counsel costs thousands of dollars. Please give me an estimate of how much you have spent on the legal counsel". "I am a legal advisor ... I would offer legal advice to AWARE *pro bono*. If you had asked for help, you would have been able to obtain free legal advice. Did you ask?" "... Such a large sum of money overspent ... Do we report this to the Commissioner of Charities?" "As an NGO, we struggle hard to get money. Now $90,000 is gone!" With every comment, the crowd roared.

Two other key issues were also raised by those in the queue — sex education and homosexuality. Someone spoke up clearly for comprehensive sex education (CSE) — its scope and merits, such as the delay of the onset of sexual activity and promotion of safer sexual activity and behaviour leading to decrease in sexually-transmitted diseases, so "I don't understand why you want to impede or discredit such a programme and give out such a lot of misinformation to lots of parents. As a parent myself, I would like my child to go through this programme ... Discussing a wide range of sexual behaviour and practices does not make one a homosexual...." Lau responded with the stress on and recommendation of abstinence from a US (Utah-based) study, and the importance of a balanced view between abstinence and CSE, noting that AWARE's sexuality education programme did not stress abstinence enough and preferred to emphasise choice. One trainer for AWARE's sexuality education programme clarified that the three words — anal sex, homosexuality and lesbianism — are mentioned in one and a half minutes out of the three-hour programme of which half is spent on abstinence. Some homosexual men and lesbian women came out in the open to say how unhappy they were with the new guard's and Thio's comments on homosexuality and imposition of their values on AWARE. Lau's reply was that homosexuals seeking help from AWARE would be referred to in-house trained counsellors, that her team will stand with lesbians who are discriminated against, and that it was for pro-choice but an informed pro-choice. Again, Lau's clarifications were too late and lost in the raging storm.

The storm moved on to sharp criticisms of the new guard's leadership competence, culture and credibility, which seemed to pelt them like hailstones. "As a member of civil society, we debate openly. We do not shut the doors on anybody. You need to be taught how to debate in civil society. You have not shown us that when you took over the organisation." "Leadership is not by position only, leadership has to earn respect. If you have no prior experience in AWARE, how do you expect to get respect?" "As a leadership team, I expect you to be familiar with the Constitution. If for every single thing you have to refer to your legal counsel who is an outsider, how are you going to lead?" One lightning shot was this comment: "I see a fundamental clash of cultures ... What I see in you is a representative of the corporate ethos, $90,000 spent in less than two months ... As an NGO, money is very tight and very important ... we reach out to anyone and any organisation ... You bring an open cheque book ... this clash of cultures, corporate culture versus NGO culture ... NGO work is about consensus, inclusiveness, with no recognition. Power is not an imperative ... you just don't understand how an NGO works!"[8]

Equally powerful and perhaps most damning to the new guard were the outpourings from the floor on the attitude and treatment of others: no courtesy of reply, lack of trust, top down authority and poor treatment of volunteers. "If you were more inclusive or transparent, I would not have resigned in the first place. I've been excluded from information, meetings." "[In the press] You wondered why we are so angry, but from the beginning, you are the ones who erased our voices ... we are not causing any physical harm and you are asking security to remove us ... how can I respect you when you are treating me like a child? And you are so rude to us. How can I believe that you are going to campaign for equality for women when you don't treat us equally?" "... I never felt the need to join AWARE because I trust it in the hands of intelligent women ... but recently I felt I have to join AWARE because I am alarmed that it should fall into the hands of a group of women which I have absolutely no confidence in at all. I listened to how they talk, they can't even answer in completeness and I asked myself what is going to happen to the good work of AWARE to land up with a group like this? This is worrying, so I decided to pay $40, line up for two hours just for one purpose — to cast my vote of NO CONFIDENCE!" This short spontaneous spurt served as the peak point and killer lightning bolt in the storm: "I feel very sad to come to a women's organisation meeting and be told to shut up and sit down.

Today is the time to stand up and speak out, not shut up and sit down!"
The applause was deafening and seemed to last forever.

The storm was so intense, the floodgates opened to let out huge
emotional torrents of anger and disgust. The SMS-ers seemed to have
forgotten to send out the message "Keep Calm Stay Dignified". I was so
engrossed with observation that I forgot to speak. When I did remember,
I saw that the queue for questioning was so long and did not feel the
need to do so. Let them speak, I thought. This was spontaneous. I
finally lined up when the queue grew short, and spoke as a founding
member and as a Christian. I said: "... On these grounds [leadership's
takeover, style and ideologies on sexuality and spousal relations], I
believe your Exco's leadership sets dangerous precedents for AWARE,
for civil society, and for Singapore society: of disregarding and disre-
specting the culture of trust, due process, openness and transparency
that has taken time to root and which others have worked so hard
to develop ... your Exco's leadership has also set back the good name
and good work of Christianity. It has also set back the constructive
processes of dialogue and collaboration between Christians, secularists
and those of other beliefs that have taken a long time to root and
painstaking efforts and processes to evolve in our highly diverse
Singapore...." I noticed that hardly anyone else from either side spoke
up as Christians (although the new guard's supporters later circulated
letters about the EGM to fellow Christians). Two spoke up as Muslims
— one as a minority concerned with the new guard's lack of diversity
representation, and another as a Muslim father who wanted comprehensive sexual education for his daughters. One Buddhist clarified that
in Buddhism, heterosexuality and homosexuality are equally accepted.

The vote counting took an unexpectedly long time because of
the three votes. This only served to prolong the attacks on the new
guard members who sat looking impassioned most of the time. I told
someone I was beginning to feel sorry for them and that they might
be traumatised, and she said, "maybe they believe they are being
martyred". The voting results were finally announced only four hours
after the votes were cast (and after a lashing storm): Resolution 3a—
1,414 for yes, 761 for no; resolution 3b—1,412 for yes, 762 for no;
resolution 3c—1,419 for yes, 755 for no. With each announcement, the
old guard's supporters whooped for joy. Placards were whipped out
and waved wildly in the air. The crowd began to chant "We are AWARE!
We are AWARE! We are AWARE!"

In the wake of the voting results, old guard member Thomas asked the Exco to resign graciously: "… Exco always remains subordinate to the members in general meetings … you no longer have the moral authority for AWARE". Lau replied: "Strictly speaking, such a resolution would have no legal effect. The Exco will consider whether to carry on in office…." I could not help thinking: "What?! Another unexpected round? Come on!" And indeed, another unexpected round of performance took place. The old guard's supporters began to chant "Resign! Resign! Resign!" One speaker challenged the Exco: "You have not only lost in the court of law, but in the court of opinion, so PLEASE JUST GO!" The old guard's legal counsel reinforced the call, citing Article 9 of the constitution. Old guard member Constance Singam gave the Exco just five minutes to consider resigning, and it turned to its legal counsel for advice. He said: "We opine the no confidence motion has no legal effect. The Exco can continue in the office if the resolution is passed … But … it is only common courtesy, customary wisdom and common sense that members resign after losing in a vote of no confidence." Old guard supporters erupted into wild cheers. It seemed even the legal counsel knew better what to do. The new guard requested and was granted ten minutes to consider resignation or continued office, in a separate room.

Meanwhile, the old guard's legal team, obviously well-prepared and aware that strategically speed was of the essence, moved to file a motion to remove the Exco should they decide not to resign and for an election to select a replacement committee if the motion was passed. Needless to say, the motion was passed with much cheering from supporters. By then, nearly half an hour had passed but there was no sign of the new guard's return. They were each called, by name and Exco position, to resume their seats at the meeting. They still did not appear and even their legal counsel did not know their whereabouts. With that, at 8.45 p.m. sharp, the old guard declared that the Exco had resigned. The supporters broke into thunderous shrieks. The team next moved rapidly to the motion that "the entire Exco is removed from office and a new Exco is to be elected", by show of hands. There were only two objections and the motion was passed. Voting of the replacement committee by show of hands took place equally quickly. The old guard had obviously lined up their nominations which were speedily made and seconded, with Dana Lam as President and a mix of old and new members. With that swift move, leadership passed back into old guard's hands. The jubilation was simply astounding. And then, just as I was thinking, "Wow! What an ending!", the new guard reappeared! The two Excos on the same stage was a surreal sight. In another situation, they could have been stretched out to each other to shake hands or embrace. I thought the performance would take yet another unexpected turn. But this time Lau said: "... The Exco has decided to graciously step down ... and we wish AWARE all the best in its future endeavours." The outburst of joy of AWARE supporters seemed to hit the roof and spread out like fireworks.

Performance Reviewed

"This beats a soccer match!" (blogger 1)

"Don't mess around with women on a mission!" (blogger 2)

"This is the best political show I have seen for a long time!" (retired journalist)

"I am so impressed with the organisation based on sheer volunteerism!" (ex-political detainee)

"I am so proud to be woman! Women are so smart!" (middle-aged observer)

"... I cried for Josie Lau and her team ... for all Christians and for the Church ... for Singapore ... for our children ... I witnessed a 'massacre'" (letter writer to the President of the National Council of Churches in Singapore)

"This is historic, eh?" (young Suntec City Convention Hall cleaner)

From my viewpoint as an insider-outsider observer, the AWARE saga is an exemplary case study of two groups, diametrically opposed in styles and values, caught in a struggle for power and legitimacy in the world of gender and civil society politics in Singapore. It was also a struggle that captured and expressed so poignantly several significant dimensions of diversity in Singapore society and showed how these can be played out publicly in dramatic and unprecedented fashion at a momentous event.

The old guard thought it would lose the battle numbers-wise but would win the war righting a wrong when well prepared. The new guard never comprehended why it was already losing the war from the very start, as it saw itself legitimately elected, and seemed not to even realise it was digging its own grave at each turning point of the battle. Its defensive position saw it take to desperate and sometimes absurd measures. It was also a performance which, once started, assumed a life of its own in which the audience often took over with on-the-spot composed "scripts". While some had come merely to watch, others were determined to have their say or were aroused to participate on stage.

The EGM has been portrayed as rowdy, raucous and rambunctious, particularly among the old guard's supporters, and indeed it bordered on the uncivil on several occasions. There were also some elements present who cared less for calm and dignity or for AWARE and more for their venting their anger, such as when Thio spoke so insensitively. Here, the specific role of the old guard's volunteers in queue- and crowd-control and in averting potential chaos was crucial. On the other hand, the new guard's supporters were quiet, indeed unexpectedly so, and many "red shirts" left after voting without even waiting for the outcome. One had to be there to witness the passion and conviction of those who believed they were righting a wrong, and to understand the emotions aroused by the other side's incivilities and insensitivities, considered so antithetical to civil society as well as to the normal sense of fair play — switching off of microphones, highhanded and disrespectful behaviour, appropriation of the achievements of others, legitimation through legalism and establishment credentialism, cheque book mentality, storm trooper tactics, and the one biggest uncivil act of all — the unethical infiltration of AWARE. The spontaneity of mass participation by the old guard's supporters was due not to ideological manipulation but pure reaction to such incivilities, and they came of their own free will. If the new guard legitimated its takeover of AWARE through legalistic means at the AGM, exploiting constitutional loopholes and slipping in new membership, the old guard now did the same for its take-back of AWARE, through a legally requisited EGM, constitutional provisions and call for new membership support and volunteers. The stark difference was that the takeover was quiet and covert while the take-back was noisy and open for all to see.

As public performance of civil society, the EGM highlighted many dimensions of leadership, organisation, volunteerism and mass participation, qualities and rules of NGO engagement, and issues and quality of debate. In these, it showed that the old guard was far superior and better prepared. In contrast, the new guard simply did not have the experience or framework to handle the intricacies of running an

NGO and the complexities of navigating civil society space. Some have attributed this to their old-line corporate culture (hierarchical, legalistic and credentialist)[9] and religious (exclusivist and obedient/unquestioning) outlooks. In the qualities and rules of engagement, it also highlighted the practices and expectations of transparency, trust, consultation, openness and volunteerism which the new guard failed to undertake or meet up to.

Contrary to common perception, the AWARE saga was not "petty politics" and a women's "catfight" internal to the organisation. It might have been more of an internal issue or concerned more specific sectors of civil society had the battle been over the (mis)appropriation of the terms "feminist" and "feminism" by Thio and the new guard for their own agenda on sex education and homosexuality. The patriarchal and dismissive "catfight and petty politics" view misses out what the AWARE saga raises and implies for civil society and indeed for Singapore society. At heart were many issues and values all worth "fighting" about — leadership, governance, transparency, civility, ethics, inclusivity, trust, rights, sexuality, conservatism, liberalism, political participation and rules of engagement, volunteerism, religion in the public domain, inter-religious relations, and state intervention.

The performance has ended but there may be others to come, perhaps again in unexpected ways. Many post-EGM developments have been taking place that point to the building up of divisive walls rather than connective bridges, particularly through cyberspace.[10] The situation continues to be a highly fluid and dynamic one. And amidst the cacophonous confusion of collective behaviour and public debate, there is bound to be disruptive behaviour. Such disruption tends to be equated with mob, raucous, uncouth and uncivil behaviour, con-tentious and divisive tendencies, and suggesting society's breakdown or society under threat. All the more in orderly Singapore that has not witnessed political and social protest for several decades. But disruption can also be positive and valuable to Singapore's public life as it forces society to pause and consider what it is doing and where it is going.[11] The AWARE EGM is one such disruption, alerting and asking Singa-poreans to ask important questions about their social lives. At the same time, it also asks how such a positive disruption can be a peaceful and constructive feature of Singapore's progress towards mature democracy, in which the public sphere needs to be enriched with social capital, trust and democratic communication skills, imbued with imagination and conviction yet not succumbing to dogmatism or tribalism.[12] The

EGM showed just how challenging this can be in the highly diverse, dynamic and complex milieu of Singapore's multicultural society.

AWARE in 1985 and AWARE in 2009 are important events in the history of civil society and public life in Singapore. Both capture the imagination of people and carry symbolic value. In 1985, AWARE was formed as one of the first civil society organisations in a context of strong state and social authoritarianism. It was guided by what was thought as right, fair and good. It did not obey the traditional authoritarian "shut up and sit down" reproach but built up the "stand up and speak out" approach, and in doing so has made many contributions to Singapore women and society. The AWARE in 2009 showed that this spirit was alive and kicking when it "booted out" unacceptable ethics and practices. In doing so, it also debunked the myths that Singaporeans are politically apathetic and that Singapore's public life is uneventful, as its impact reverberated through discussions among groups and individuals long after. The vehement passion, conviction and courage with which AWARE fights for what is right, fair and good portend well. For women, for civil society and for Singapore, the greatest gain from the AWARE saga is the reminder not to shut up and sit down but to stand up and speak out.

Notes

1. This is an ethnographic and first person account by an insider-outsider participant observer. As a founding and life member of AWARE, I am an "insider" who became involved in the saga after reading media reports of the "new guard", viewing their performance at their first press conference, and hearing the confession of their "feminist mentor". My dormant sense of activism was awoken and I became convinced I had to rise to the occasion. As an "outsider", I attempt to view the EGM through the lens of a social anthropologist with working knowledge and experience of inter-ethnic, intercultural and interfaith issues and dynamics. While my anthropological analysis benefited from my "insider" status such as being made privy to some close-door meetings, I am aware of the fact that this very "insider" status denied my access to the other side. My description and interpretation of the EGM here are based on my own subjective experiences, observations, recollection, limited insider access and data collected from various media sources. I am certain there will be questions as to my credibility to write about the EGM, especially given my involvement on one side. The first person account is a valid approach in social inquiry,

including in gender studies and feminist theory. I believe anyone who attended the EGM is qualified to write about it, provided he/she accounts openly and honestly for her interest and position in it. But even as I am an AWARE life member, the responsibility for views expressed here is solely mine.

2. According to my informant, one AWARE member at the AGM recalled an earlier conversation that she had with X, in which X asked if the Christians had already taken over AWARE. X said that she had been asked to join a group of Christians to take over AWARE as they felt it had become pro-gay, but X declined. At the AGM, this member recalled the conversation and told some AWARE members, and these members discretely searched the Internet on the new candidates and found that some of them had written anti-homosexual letters to the press.

3. *The Straits Times*, "Lawyer's Key Role in Aware Coup", 24 April 2009.

4. *The Straits Times*, "Church Against Homosexuality as 'Normal Alternative Lifestyle'", 1 May 2009, p. A6.

5. *The Straits Times*, "Churches Should Stay Out of AWARE Tussle", 1 May 2009 and "Pastor regrets 'actions on pulpit'", 2 May 2009.

6. I later heard that one of the new guard's husbands had taken over the hall's sound system from the Suntec City's technician.

7. Old guard Braema Mathi later told me that she feared a skirmish as some angry people inched closer to Thio who went on with her speech. Mathi asked a security officer to tell Josie Lau to stop Thio, but as Lau did not, she led her section of supporters to start chanting "We are AWARE!" to diffuse the high tension. To her, this episode crystallised the struggle: "Thio with her beliefs against homosexuality, speaking with such self-righteousness versus the gay women who were hissing in anger and sorrow at the self-denial imposed on them."

8. I later heard that when the new guard left the stage to decide whether to resign or to continue, it quickly signed cheques to pay for whatever outstanding amounts it had incurred for which it now incurred wrath. However, the restored old guard later negotiated with the various vendors to write off or offer discounts, and did not take further legal action against the new guard.

9. Tan Dan Feng, "Being Culturally Aware", <http://www.we-are-aware.sg/tags/danfeng/>.

10. Both sides have received hate mail. An e-petition by a "conservative majority" called for the Ministry of Education (MOE) to withdraw AWARE's sexuality education programme in secondary schools (which it did just a week after the EGM, in a turnaround policy, see *The Straits Times*, 29 April 2009). In one circulated e-document *Understanding the Broader Issues*, "liberalism" is identified as the main ideological enemy as it purportedly promotes liberal sexuality, liberal lifestyles and liberal

morality. Others focus specifically on homosexuality and LBGTQ (lesbian, bisexual, gay, transgender, queer) and have sent letters to parents of adolescents alerting them to their growing trends in Singapore and calling for the setting up of a lobby group, even though the MOE and social workers have identified the main problems with adolescents' sexuality to be premature sex and sexually transmitted diseases, not homosexuality. They also warn the public that some AWARE members and supporters are actively setting up other civil society organisations.

11.   Kenneth Paul Tan, "Singapore's Active Citizens: Finding a Way between Dogmatism and Uncritical Pragmatism", *Global-is-Asian*, Issue 4 (Oct./Dec. 2009).

12.   Ibid.

References

Association of Women for Action and Research, Information pack for EGM, 2 May 2009.

Culver, Sheldon and John Dorhauer, 2007, *Steeplejacking: How the Christian Right is Hijacking Mainstream Religion*. Brooklyn: Ig Publishing.

Lai Ah Eng, Personal notes and transcripts of the AWARE EGM on 2 May 2009.

————, 2008, *Religious Diversity in Singapore*. Singapore: Institute of Policy Studies and Institute of Southeast Asian Studies.

Tan Dan Feng, "Being Culturally Aware" <http://www.we-are-aware.sg/tags/danfeng/> [accessed 1 Oct. 2009].

Tan, Kenneth Paul, Oct./Dec. 2009, "Singapore's Active Citizens: Finding a Way between Dogmatism and Uncritical Pragmatism", *Global-is-Asian*, Issue 4.

The Straits Times, "Lawyer's Key Role in Aware Coup".

————, 24 April 2009, "No Complaints from Parents, Dr Thio".

————, 1 May 2009, "Churches Should Stay Out of AWARE Tussle".

————, 1 May 2009, "Church Against Homosexuality as 'Normal Alternative Lifestyle'".

————, 2 May 2009, "Pastor regrets 'actions on pulpit'".

The Wayang Party, LIVE from Suntec: AWARE EGM, 2 May 2009. <http://wayangparty.com/?p=8732> [accessed 1 June 2009].

Understanding the Broader Issues (unnamed and undated).

CHAPTER 10

AWARE Re-pluralised, Re-secularised: Transition to Deeper Awareness

Vivienne Wee[1]

The Association of Women for Action and Research (AWARE) is Singapore's only self-declared feminist organisation, as distinct from a women's organisation. Lyons (2004: 145) noted:

> While it is true that no other equivalent "feminist" organisation exists in Singapore, women's organisations, including those that focus on improving the lives of women, abound. However, these associations tend to be based on "race" or religion.

Among women's organisations in Singapore, AWARE has thus been unique in its dedication to the promotion of gender equality, irrespective of "race" or religion. This stance implies secularity and plurality, although no explicit statement concerning such matters was ever made by the organisation in its first 24 years. AWARE became explicit about its adherence to secularity and plurality only after the occurrence of a sequence of events in 2009 variously dubbed "the AWARE hijacking", "the AWARE coup", "the AWARE saga", or "the AWARE affair" by the media, bloggers and academic observers.

On 18 April 2009, three weeks after the takeover of AWARE by the so-called "new guard", *The Straits Times* did an exposé in two key articles.[2] The article titled "Some attend the same church" revealed that all the five new office-bearers, as well as one of the four Exco members, were from the Anglican Church of Our Saviour at Margaret Drive.

This article also revealed that Lau's husband, Dr Alan Chin, "is related to former law dean Dr Thio Su Mien and her daughter, Nominated Member of Parliament Professor Thio Li-Ann", and that Thio Su Mien and her husband also attend the same church. Significantly, Thio Li-Ann had spoken out in Singapore Parliament in October 2007 to support the continuing criminalisation of homosexual relations between men, laid out in 377A of the Penal Code, as inherited from Victorian legislation.[3]

After the exposé in *The Straits Times*, the newly-elected AWARE Exco decided to hold a press conference on 23 April 2009, where Thio Su Mien described herself as a "feminist mentor" of the women elected to AWARE's Exco at the AGM. Thio expressed her concern about the threat she perceived in homosexuality, which had led her to collect and email information about this to different people. In 2008, when she saw that only 29 people attended AWARE's AGM, she started encouraging the women she was mentoring to join AWARE, because she saw AWARE's Comprehensive Sexuality Education Programme (CSE) as promoting homosexuality. While she lauded AWARE for having "done great work [for women] in so many areas", she said that she was dismayed to find that "AWARE seems to be only very interested [in] the advancement of homosexuality, which is a man's issue and how it came under AWARE is quite covert." She stated that she has "nothing against lesbians or homosexuals personally", but has counselled them and think that "they are in pain", very often because of "abusive fathers, [who] do things with their daughters and the daughters revolt, rebel against society". Therefore, she saw the mission of her "friends" in the newly-elected Exco as making AWARE "go back to *look after the majority, all women, all women of Singapore*" [my italics]. Thio's view was echoed by the members of the newly-elected Exco.[4]

In response, on 24 April 2009, the older members of AWARE, now dubbed "the old guard" by the media, issued a press statement, which staked out an explicit position on pluralism:[5]

> We are glad that the truth is finally out. What happened at [the] AWARE AGM on 28 March was a planned takeover by a group of women, guided by their "feminist mentor" Dr Thio Su Mien, who have taken it upon themselves to, as they put it, "bring AWARE back to its original, very noble, objective".
>
> The issue is not whether AWARE has indeed strayed from its original aims. What is really at stake is the space for a diversity of views in our cosmopolitan and pluralistic society. Singapore is a multiracial, multireligious and multicultural society. As we progress,

the diversity will grow. We have to be able to co-exist, to live with differing views on many issues.

What has happened at AWARE is a threat to Singapore's pluralistic society.... [This] cannot be the way forward for Singapore. We cannot have people acting like moral vigilantes running around and taking over established organisations. If Dr Thio and her mentees feel that AWARE has strayed from its original aims, or that some of the programmes are unsuitable, then go ahead and criticize AWARE, but do so openly.

The older members of AWARE also held a press conference on the same day, 24 April 2009, again emphasising the plural all-inclusive character of the organisation.[6] They identified the key defining characteristic of pluralism as "space for ... diversity".

The fault-line between two groups was now clear. The view of the older members was that AWARE's pluralism provided "space for ... diversity" and included all women, irrespective of "race, religion and *sexuality*" [my italics], as stated during the 28 March 2009 AGM. In contrast, the view of the newcomers was that AWARE should "look after *the majority, all women, all women of Singapore*" [my italics], to quote the "feminist mentor" Thio. This difference of views was quickly noted by letter writers to the forum page of *The Straits Times*, who expressed concern about the latter's "exclusionary stance". For example, letter writer Dionne Sok Ling Thompson argued that "women who discriminate against other women should not lead an organisation meant to help all women" (*The Straits Times* 25 April 2009).[7]

The newcomers' assertion that only a heterosexual majority represents "all women" implies that this majority excludes a homosexual minority. This assertion is of the same fabric as the argument presented in Parliament on 22 October 2007 by Thio Li-Ann, Thio Su Mien's daughter, when she argued in favour of continuing to criminalise homosexual relations between men, because "while homosexuals are a numerical minority, there is no such thing as 'sexual minorities' at law".[8] It was this connection that had prompted Thio Su Mien to say on 23 April 2009 that "the advancement of homosexuality ... is a man's issue [*sic*]",[9] implying that homosexuality is not a women's issue or rather, not an issue of "the majority" representing "all women".[10]

The debate about who is included in "all" was in fact seeded in the Parliamentary debate in October 2007 over the petition to repeal the law Section 377A that criminalises homosexual relations between men. In his critique of Thio Li-Ann, Janadas Devan pointed out that her view of pluralism "means that under certain circumstances — to be determined by whatever passes for the majority at any moment, I suppose — pluralism can insist on a singular 'ultimate principle or kind of being'".

The claim that a majority can rightfully exclude a minority the former regards as illegitimate was addressed in an interesting way by letter writer Jarel Seeh, who noted that "the majority religion in Singapore is Buddhism, at 42.5 per cent. Christianity weighs in at 14.6 per cent" (*The Straits Times* 25 April 2009).[11] Yet it is those who are from this minority religion who wish to exclude another minority in Singapore. Therefore, beneath the claim that a majority has the right to exclude a minority is another claim that a self-appointed group of people can represent this putative majority. In other words, there was not only a claim about who is to be included in "all", but also a claim about who *speaks* for "all".

On what basis can a small group claim to represent "all"? We may discern the basis of such a claim from Thio Li-Ann's speech in Parliament in October 2007:

> Religious views are part of our common morality. We separate 'religion' from 'politics', but not 'religion' from 'public policy'. That would be undemocratic. All citizens may propose views in public debate, whether influenced by religious or secular convictions or both; only the government can impose a view by law. Incidentally, one does not have to be religious to consider homosexuality contrary to biological design and immoral....

Thio Li-Ann thus purported to speak on behalf of "religious views", without acknowledging that there is diversity within any one religion, as well as between religions. She further claimed that "to be religious [is] to consider homosexuality contrary to biological design and immoral", a position that, she says, is also shared by some of those who are not religious.

The moral voice that is asserted thus claims to speak on behalf of (i) all heterosexuals, (ii) all Christians, and (iii) all religious people. As argued by Thio Li-Ann, her particular "religious views" are supposed to be "part of *our common morality*" (my italics). There was awareness on the part of various members of the public of the need to rebut such claims. For example, letter writer Jarel Seeh felt the need to declare herself as "not a homosexual" who respects "the rights of minority groups ... [who] exist in the real world [and] are people, like you and me". She stated: "It is wrong to invalidate their presence and rights."[12] Another letter writer, Ace Kindred Cheong, wrote: "I have many gay and lesbian friends. I do not detest them because I know they have their reasons for being what they are. Again, having gay and lesbian friends does not mean I am encouraged to be a gay."[13] The "old guard" of AWARE also affirmed that while they recognise "the heterosexual family [as] the norm for our society", they also recognise homosexuals as "part of our society [who] should be able to live freely and happily, free of any discrimination".[14]

To rebut the claim that all Christians discriminate against homo-sexuals, a gay Christian website in Singapore provided 12 web pages of commentaries on what it referred to as "the AWARE revolution".[15] Letters were written by some members of the public to rebut the claim that all religious people discriminate against homosexuals. For example, letter writer Soh Chin Ong opined that homosexuality "is a sin only in the Judeo-Christian framework, not in Buddhism or Hinduism".[16]

The question of who speaks for whom is central to pluralism. At the heart of pluralism is the notion that people must speak for them-selves in plural voices, expressing diverse views. This was the implicit plurality embraced by older members of AWARE, expressed not just in their press statement of 24 April 2009 (see above), but also in their explanation about the Comprehensive Sexuality Education Programme (CSE), which Thio Su Mien and her mentees regarded as promoting homosexuality. Concerning CSE, Constance Singam, former president of AWARE, explained "that the programme was a comprehensive one, designed to provide teens with information in a non-judgmental way. 'We do not teach kids to impart judgment, we just give them information,' she said. 'Their values come from their family, and their religion. Words like 'homosexuality', 'sexy' and 'virginity' are neutral words because AWARE is non-judgmental" (*The Straits Times* 27 April 2009).[17] "Non-judgmental information" is a stance adopted to com-municate multiple perspectives so that the student can form his or her own informed judgement — a position congruent with a pedagogical approach that encourages students to think for themselves with whatever diverse results that may ensue.[18]

The question of who speaks for whom is also central to feminism. All too often, women's voices are silenced by those who claim to speak for them, including fathers, husbands, brothers, male leaders, and the like. The silencing process is compounded for women who are disadvantaged economically, educationally, politically, socially or in other ways. Hawkesworth (2003: 2–3) provided a brief overview of the emergence of "the politics of representation" in feminist discourse:

> The politics of representation has been and continues to be central to feminist activism and scholarship. Political contestations concerning the claims made on behalf of women, the conditions under which such claims are made, who makes the claims and for whom they are made, and whose interests are served by particular articulations of women's needs and interests have been a staple of feminist debates. *The politics of representation was initially introduced to the feminist agenda by voices from the margin speaking in their own behalf* [my italics]. African American women contested the priorities and lack of inclusiveness of movements led by white women's rights activists in the 19th and 20th centuries in the United States; lesbian feminists challenged homophobia and heteronormativity in second wave feminism; "Third World women" repudiated the racial, ethnic, nationalist and class biases circulating in transnational feminist networks.

World-wide, there has been increasing convergence of feminism and pluralism, such that feminist pluralism is now accepted as a necessary locus for discourses on human rights, multi-culturalism, and socio-economic development.[19] In the context of AWARE in Singapore, however, the events of March to May 2009 saw an attempt by some Christian women to reverse this trend by trying to reduce the politics of representation through the exclusion of lesbians as "women".[20]

Although the question of who speaks for whom was not explicitly debated, this issue nevertheless resonated strongly with older members of AWARE. Such resonance may be discerned in a famous incident that occurred during the Extraordinary General Meeting (EGM) of 2 May 2009 that had been requested by 150 members of AWARE, as constitutionally allowed, so that members could vote on a motion of no confidence in the new Exco.[21] At one point during the EGM, one of the newcomers on AWARE's Exco, Sally Ang, tried to silence speakers on the floor by saying "Shut up and sit down!" When she said this, uproar burst from the audience, who, at that moment, seemed to have recognised this as an articulation of the silencing intent of the newcomers.

So significant was this utterance that a shaky blurred video-recording of the moment has been uploaded on YouTube by a blogger.[22] After the newcomers resigned their positions during the EGM and the "old guard" regained control over AWARE, a supporter of the latter who was not at the EGM, Vicki Lew, felt moved to produce T-shirts that displayed the words "shut up and sit down" on the front.[23] There is even a song called "Shut up and sit down — the AWARE saga remixed", produced by an anonymous supporter by remixing quotations from the EGM, with a chorus singing "shut up, shut up" repeatedly in the background.[24] Another song, also called "Shut up and sit down", has been composed and performed on stage in September 2009 by Rosie and the Pussycat Dolls in the comedy *The (Extraordinary) V Conference*.[25] The significance of this imperative phrase has reverberated at least up to August 2010, when, at a meeting to discuss the celebration of AWARE's 25th anniversary, president Dana Lam explicitly said that AWARE's current aim is to encourage women to stand up and speak out (pers. comm.).

Like one who belatedly realises that she has been speaking prose all her life, the new-old AWARE after the EGM arrived at a deeper organisational self-awareness of its adherence to pluralism and secularism. As shown above, the older members of AWARE affirmed their adherence to pluralism as "space for a diversity of views". In the period March to May 2009, although they had also identified themselves as being "secular", there was, at that time, no elaboration of what this means. In a letter to AWARE members, dated 19 April 2009, former president Constance Singam wrote, "AWARE is a secular organisation that embraces diversity of race, age, religion, culture and sexuality, and it must remain so."[26] And at the press conference organised by them on 24 April 2009, former president Kanwaljit Soin said, "It is incumbent upon us to be secular ... AWARE is secular and it will remain so."[27]

It was only since May 2010 that AWARE commenced discussion in earnest about what being secular means. On 20 May 2010, Singam wrote an article for AWARE's website, titled "State's decisions a threat to secular society", in which she criticised the Singapore Government for deviating from "its determination to protect the secular nature of our society [by] privileging one system of values over other value systems and in so doing is in danger of subverting the very nature of a secular society". What she was referring to was the Ministry of Education's "choice of vendors to teach sex education in schools [with] four of the six approved ... known to be part of conservative Christian groups" as well as "the National Art Commission's decision to cut the funding of theatre group Wild Rice because, the Commission said, it would not fund 'projects which are incompatible with the core values promoted by the government'".[28]

Singam quoted Stephen Law's discussion of "a secular society" as one that "protects certain freedoms. It protects the freedom of individuals to believe, or not believe, to worship, or not worship.... It is founded on principles framed and justified independently of any particular pro- or anti-religious commitment: principles to which we ought to be able to sign up whether we are religious or not."[29] Significantly, on 15 May 2009, when the Deputy Prime Minister, Wong Kan Seng, expressed the Government's worry "about the disquieting public perception that a group of conservative Christians, all attending the same church, which held strong views on homosexuality, had moved in and taken over AWARE because they disapproved of what AWARE had been doing", he also presented a view that was not very different from Law's characterisation:

> We are a secular Singapore, in which Christians, Muslims, Buddhists, Hindus and others all have to live in peace with one another. This calls for tolerance, accommodation, and give and take on all sides. If religious groups start to campaign to change certain government policies, or use the pulpit to mobilise their followers to pressure the government, or push aggressively to gain ground at the expense of other groups, this must lead to trouble. Keeping religion and politics separate is a key rule of political engagement.... Our political arena must always be a secular one. Our laws and policies do not derive from religious authority, but reflect the judgments and decisions of the secular Government and Parliament to serve the national interest and collective good. *These laws and public policies apply equally to all, regardless of one's race, religion or social status. This gives confidence that the system will give equal treatment and protection for all, regardless of which group one happens to belong to.*[30] [my italics]

It would seem that Wong's "laws and public policies [that] apply equally to all, regardless of one's race, religion or social status" are not unlike Law's founding "principles framed and justified independently of any particular pro- or anti-religious commitment: principles to which we ought to be able to sign up whether we are religious or not".

The Government's view was elaborated upon by the Prime Minister, Lee Hsien Loong, in his National Day Rally Speech on 16 August 2009:[31]

> ... The Government has to remain secular. The Government's authority comes from the people. The laws are passed by Parliament which is elected by the people. They don't come from a sacred book. *The Government has to be neutral, fair.* [my italics] *...We hold the ring*

so that all groups can practise their faiths freely without colliding.
[my italics]

... Religious groups are free to propagate their teachings on social and moral issues. They have done so on the IRs, organ transplants, 377A, homosexuality....

... When people who have a religion approach a national issue, they will often have views which are informed by their religious beliefs.... *But you must accept that other groups may have different views informed by different beliefs and you have to accept that and respect that. The public debate cannot be on whose religion is right and whose religion is wrong. It has to be on secular, rational considerations of public interest — what makes sense for Singapore.* [my italics]

The final requirement for us to live peacefully together is to maintain our common space that all Singaporeans share. It has to be *neutral and secular* because that's the only way all of us can feel at home in Singapore and at ease. [my italics]

... We were not concerned about who would control AWARE because it's just one of so many NGOs in Singapore. On homosexuality policy or sexuality education in schools, there can be strong differences in view but the Government's position was quite clear.... But what worried us was that this was an attempt by a religiously motivated group who shared a strong religious fervour to enter civil space, take over an NGO it disapproved of, and impose their agenda. It was bound to provoke a push back from groups that held the opposite view, which indeed happened vociferously and stridently....

... *This was hardly the way to conduct a mature discussion of a sensitive matter where views are deeply divided. But most critically of all, this risked a broader spillover into relations between different religions.*

The framework presented by the Prime Minister makes a distinction between a secular state where the Government has to be secular, neutral and fair, holding the ring "so that all groups can practise their faiths freely without colliding" and a multi-religious society where "religious groups are free to propagate their teachings on social and moral issues", on the condition that they accept and respect "that other groups may have different views informed by different beliefs". What seems to be problematic in this framework is how differences are to be negotiated. Is it just a matter of "not colliding" in a ring held by a neutral and fair Government? In the last paragraph quoted above, the Prime Minister referred to a need for "mature" discussions of divided views. What conditions are needed for such "mature" discussions? Is there a neutral and fair discursive space that allows the negotiation of differences without such discussions being pre-empted or cut off as collisions in the making?

The need for a discursive space that allows the expression of diverse views, even if not yet a negotiation of differences, seems to be keenly felt by AWARE members after the organisation regained its secular character. A significant recent development is the organising of monthly AWARE Roundtables as a regular discursive space. Significantly, apart from more usual women's issues, such as violence against women, the topics chosen for discussion include fundamentalisms (not only in Singapore but also elsewhere in the region), secularity and secularism, as well as women's citizenship in the public sphere. As stated on AWARE's website, although "discussion and debate have always been an important part of AWARE", there is now a felt need "to make this discussion and debate a regular activity with a more formal structure, with a key aim [being to] strengthen AWARE's capacity to identify, understand and respond to a wide range of trends, issues and policies".[32] It is also significant that these Roundtables seem to be attracting a wider range of members of the public, other than those interested in more usual women's issues.

A more explicit realisation of AWARE's secularity was also manifested in the stand taken by the organisation in the case of Kartika, a Malaysian woman sentenced to six lashes of the cane for drinking beer. Because Kartika is also a permanent resident of Singapore, AWARE co-signed, with the Joint Action Group and Sisters in Islam of Malaysia, as well as with Solidaritas Perempuan of Indonesia, letters that were addressed to the United Nations Human Rights Commission in Geneva, including the Special Rapporteurs on Violence Against Women and on Torture. Furthermore, AWARE supports and is represented in the Southeast Asian Progressive Muslim Movement (APMM), which was formed at a regional meeting in Jakarta (16 and 17 October 2009) by several non-governmental organisations and networks in the region.

Conclusion

All these developments signify a greater self-awareness of AWARE as a secular and plural actor in civil society, such that its secularity and plurality are no longer implicit assumptions, but have developed into explicit values. Explicitness enables discourse, discussion and debate in a way that implicitness does not. This has widened the discursive space within AWARE, while enabling the organisation to take on and analyse a more extensive range of issues and thereby play a larger role in civil society.

There is now explicit recognition by AWARE members that while this discursive space accommodates diverse views and beliefs, the negotiation of differences through discourse needs to be conducted with transparency and in good faith, without hidden agendas of conversion and take-over. A by-line formulated in 2009 — "trust, respect, choice" — attempts to express this idea. As explained by President Dana Lam in June 2009 (pers. comm.), this by-line implies that people need to trust each other as "informed individuals capable of choice" who are "deserving of opportunities equal to those of men in education, marriage and employment" and who are "able to control their own bodies, particularly with regard to sexual and reproductive health".

Formalising such values as foundational to the organisation, AWARE now requires applicants for membership to declare the following in their application form:[33]

Declaration of Values and Agreement to Objectives

By submitting this application, I confirm that I am joining AWARE because I agree with its objectives, and specifically:

1. I share AWARE's vision of gender equality and support the aim of creating awareness of the mutual rights and responsibilities of women and men.
2. I believe that the well-being of women requires a woman to have full control over her body and her fertility.
3. I agree that AWARE should embrace diversity of race, age, culture and sexuality; promote tolerance and acceptance of diversity; and respect the individual and the choices she makes in life and support her when needed. These, I agree, are values and norms which would improve the quality of life of women and their families and achieve the betterment of Singapore society as a whole.

This required declaration has the effect of filtering out those who do not agree with these values from joining AWARE as members. For example, a former AWARE member — a self-identified Christian — told me (pers. comm.) that she was on the verge of re-joining AWARE but did not do so because of this required declaration. When I asked what she had objected to in the declaration, she said that her only problem was being asked to respect "homosexual lifestyles", even though no such words actually occur in the declaration. If her response may be taken as indicative, then it would seem that the phrase "diversity of ... sexuality" is being read by some as meaning "homosexual life-styles", which they evidently would not allow within the scope of acceptable diversity.

As stated in the press release of 24 April 2009 by the "old guard", "what is really at stake is the space for a diversity of views...."[34] In the contestation between those trying to reduce this space by excluding sexual diversity and those wanting this space to include such diversity, the latter — represented by the "old guard" — was publicly supported by other non-governmental organisations. These included Transient Workers Count Too (TWC2), Raleigh Society, International Volunteerism Association, The Necessary Stage, Humanitarian Organisation for Migration Economics (HOME), Singapore Council of Women's Organisations (SCWO) and UNIFEM Singapore.[35] This was a new phenomenon in Singapore — that is, the rallying of civil society organisations around a particular organisation whose *raison d'être* was being threatened by a "hostile take-over" by newcomers with a very different agenda, to quote from the statement of support by The Necessary Stage.[36] This wider mobilisation signifies a new awareness in civil society that values of pluralism and secularism can no longer be assumed but need to be defended and promoted. In this shift of awareness, AWARE is playing a leading role such that relations between AWARE and a wider community of civil society organisations have become closer and more mutually supportive. The expanded discursive space within AWARE thus relates to intensified dialogue across different missions and visions, based on a shared concern for the protection and development of space for diversity in a plural secular society.

Notes

1. This analysis is based primarily on information in the public domain and secondarily on information obtained through personal communication. As a founder and life member of AWARE, I am an "insider" who learnt about the events discussed in this chapter first through media reports, then through communications with some fellow members. As I was then living outside Singapore, I initiated an e-petition to protest the take-over of AWARE — "Save AWARE! Gender equality for all!" — which garnered 2,763 signatures. I am aware that my "insider" status pre-disposes me to take a view that is aligned more closely with AWARE's original mission and vision than with the view of the newcomers who took over AWARE in 2009. However, in the highly polarised situation that developed in March–May 2009, people who were involved in the contestation of views mostly took one side or

the other and were hardly neutral. But from the perspective of feminist scholarship, it is debatable whether claims of "neutrality" are ever adequately realised in social science research, since researchers generally do not declare their existing biases and prejudices. Instead, feminist researchers advocate reflexivity, *pace* Gouldner (1970), as a more realistic and more ethical approach to research, rather than to pretend that social scientists are "pure visitors" (to use Gellner's term [1964]) without any existing experiences. (Also see Archer 2000; Lemert and Piccone 1982; Levesque-Lopman 1989.) Although there is no space here to discuss "reflexivity" at length, suffice it to note that it entails self-awareness of one's social locus, the impact of that on one's perspective, and a declaration of the resulting view as emanating from that perspective. Although I am an AWARE founder and life member and although that social locus may have affected my perspective, the views expressed in this paper and any mistakes that may have inadvertently occurred are nevertheless solely mine. They do not represent the views of the organisation or of any other member in AWARE.

2.   The two articles are titled "Some attend the same church" and "Who's who at the new AWARE ... and the questions they will not answer".

3.   Section 377A ("Outrages on decency") states: "Any male person who, in public or private, commits, or abets the commission of, or procures or attempts to procure the commission by any male person of, any act of gross indecency with another male person, shall be punished with imprisonment for a term which may extend to two years." [*Singapore Penal Code*, Chapter XVI (Offences Affecting the Human Body), Section 377 (Cap. 224).]

4.   "23 Apr 2009 Press conference transcript", 24 April 2009, <http://helpsave aware.blogspot.com/2009/04/23-april-2009-press-conference.html>; also see "Excerpts from AWARE press conference", 26 April 2009, <http://www. asiaone.com/News/AsiaOne%2BNews/Singapore/Story/A1Story20090426-137518/2.html>.

5.   This press release was widely disseminated in the media and on many blogs. See, for example, "'We cannot have people acting like moral vigilantes' says AWARE's old guards", 24 April 2009, <http://theonlinecitizen. com/2009/04/we-cannot-have-people-acting-like-moral-vigilantes-says-awares-old-guards/>.

6.   "AWARE Old Guard's press conference, 24 Apr 09", *Channel News Asia*, <http://www.youtube.com/watch?v=T6zyy11ppV0>.

7.   For a discussion about whether the view of the "new guard" constitutes a type of "feminism", see chapter by Devasahayam in this volume.

8.   "377A serves public morality: NMP Thio Li-Ann", 23 Oct. 2007, <http:// theonlinecitizen.com/2007/10/377a-serves-public-morality-nmp-thio-li-ann/>.

9. "23 Apr 2009 Press conference transcript", 24 April 2009, <http://helpsave aware.blogspot.com/2009/04/23-april-2009-press-conference.html>.

10. Thio Su Mien may also have been implying that only men can possibly be homosexuals and thus advancement of homosexual rights would be, in her logic, a men's issue. Her view could have been derived from some Biblical references to male homosexual behaviour, especially Leviticus 18: 22 and Leviticus 20: 13. In contrast, there appears to be only one Biblical reference to female homosexuality — Romans 1: 26. The emphasis on male homosexuality symptomises a masculinist understanding of sexuality solely as penile penetration. Walter Wink (no date) [Professor Emeritus of Biblical Interpretation at Auburn Theological Seminary, New York], traces this to the "Hebrew prescientific understanding ... that male semen contained the whole of nascent life. With no knowledge of eggs and ovulation, it was assumed that the woman provided only the incubating space. Hence the spilling of semen for any nonprocreative purpose — in coitus interruptus (Genesis 38: 1–11), male homosexual acts, or male masturbation — was considered tantamount to abortion or murder. (Female homosexual acts were consequently not so seriously regarded, and are not mentioned at all in the Old Testament....)." This masculinist view of sexuality underlies the Victorian criminalisation of male homosexuality and not female homosexuality in Section 377A. As explained by Pearsall (1969: 576), "When the Criminal Law Amendment Act of 1885 was amended to make homosexual acts in private a crime it referred only to men — no one could think of a way to explain to Queen Victoria what homosexual acts between women were." Thio Li-Ann apparently shares this view of sex as consisting of penile penetration, equating homosexuality with sodomy (see "377A serves public morality: NMP Thio Li-Ann", 23 Oct. 2007). The ancient Hebrew criminalisation of male homosexuality was much more severe than Victorian criminalisation and called for male homosexuals to "be put to death" (Leviticus 20: 13). So if textual literalists are adhering to this verse, then by implication, they are calling not just for the criminalisation of male homosexuality but also for it to be punished by death.

11. "ST Forum: Respect minorities", 25 April 2009, <http://www.we-are-aware. sg/2009/04/25/april-25-published-st-forum-letter-by-jarel-seeh-respect-rights-of-minorities/>.

12. Ibid.

13. "ST Forum: Wrong to say old EXCO promoted homosexuality", 25 April 2009, <http://www.we-are-aware.sg/2009/04/25/ace-kindredcheong/>.

14. This was said publicly at least three times:

    • In a letter to Dr John Chew, the Anglican Bishop of Singapore, who had written in his pastoral letter to his congregation that "AWARE has an agenda 'for redefining mainstream sexual ethics and social norms' [and] that the concerns of Dr Thio Su Mien and her mentees about AWARE's direction were 'not misplaced'." See "Letter to Dr John Chew", 15 May 2009, <http://www.we-are-aware.sg/2009/05/15/letter-to-dr-john-chew/>.

- In a letter to *The Straits Times*: see "ST letter by Dana Lam: AWARE has never had a 'gay agenda'", 16 May 2009, <http://www.sgpolitics.net/?p=3029>.
- In a press statement: "AWARE: gay agenda 'unfounded'", 16 May 2009, <http://www.sgpolitics.net/?p=3029>.

15. *rainbow harvest: proclaiming God's inclusive love*, <http://www.psa91.com/>.
16. "Open letter: lessons for our secular nation", 4 May 2009, <http://www.we-are-aware.sg/2009/05/04/may-4-be-aware-lessons-for-our-secular-nation-by-ong-soh-chin/>.
17. "Why neutral stance on homosexuals", 27 April 2009, <http://www.ngejay.com/?p=2595>.
18. For example, DeLaet (2008) wrote a "pedagogical essay" where she stated that a fundamental tenet of her teaching philosophy is that students should end her course "with more questions than answers" and that "giving them the 'right answers' or guiding them to 'the truth'" was not her job. Instead she tries to provide the intellectual tools for understanding a "complex and messy" world, so that they would be less accepting of platitudes and more questioning of "boldly stated assertions".
19. The term "feminist pluralism" may be understood to mean that feminism must necessarily be plural by including all types of diversity and pluralism must necessarily be feminist by including all women.
20. Sojourner Truth's rhetorical question of 1851 "Ain't I a woman?" is evidently still relevant for Singaporean lesbians in the twenty-first century.
21. For details about AWARE's Extraordinary Meeting of 2 May 2009, please see the chapter by Lai in this volume. Also see "The AWARE saga", 2 May 2009, <http://www.we-are-aware.sg/2009/05/02/aware-saga/>.
22. "Sally Ang's 'shut up and sit down' incident at EGM", 2 May 2009, <http://www.youtube.com/watch?v=D-VYBZgwGdg>.
23. "Get your AWARE 2009 EGM T-shirts", 4 May 2009, <http://mathialee.wordpress.com/2009/05/04/get-your-aware-2009-egm-t-shirts/>.
24. <http://singapese.wordpress.com/2009/05/13/shut-up-and-sit-down-a-song-about-the-aware-egm/>.
25. "An Extraordinary V Conference", 21 July 2009, <http://www.fifo.sg/post/show/329>.
26. "TOC exclusive: Constance Singam's letter to AWARE, in full", 19 April 2009, <http://theonlinecitizen.com/2009/04/toc-exclusive-constance-singam%E2%80%99s-letter-to-aware-in-full/>.
27. "TOC breaking news: Old AWARE exco holds press conference, calls new AWARE 'moral vigilantes'", 24 April 2009, <http://theonlinecitizen.com/2009/04/toc-breaking-news-old-aware-exco-holds-press-conference-calls-new-aware-moral-vigilantes/>.

28. "State's decisions a threat to secular society", 20 May 2010, <http://www.aware.org.sg/2010/05/states-decisions-a-threat-to-secular-society/>.

29. "Humanism and secularism", 1 Jan. 2010, <http://stephenlaw.blogspot.com/search?q=freedoms>.

30. *Today*'s interview with DPM Wong Kan Seng on the AWARE saga", 15 May 2009, <http://www.sgpolitics.net/?p=3009>.

31. "Prime Minister Lee Hsien Loong's National Day Rally Speech 2009 on 16 Aug. (Transcript)", <http://www.pmo.gov.sg/News/Messages/National+Day+Rally+Speech+2009+Part+3+Racial+and+Religious+Harmony.htm>.

32. "AWARE Roundtable Discussions", 27 Aug. 2010, <http://www.aware.org.sg/2010/08/round-table/>.

33. <http://www.aware.org.sg/register/>.

34. This press release was widely disseminated in the media and on many blogs. See, for example, "'We cannot have people acting like moral vigilantes' says AWARE's old guards", 24 April 2009, <http://theonlinecitizen.com/2009/04/we-cannot-have-people-acting-like-moral-vigilantes-says-awares-old-guards/>.

35. "Statements of support from civil society groups", 30 April 2009, <http://www.we-are-aware.sg/2009/04/30/statements-of-support-from-civil-society-groups/>; also "SCWO acknowledgment of AWARE contribution", no date, <http://www.facebook.com/topic.php?uid=72296674515&topic=8006>.

36. <http://www.we-are-aware.sg/2009/04/30/statements-of-support-from-civil-society-groups/>.

References

"23 April 2009 Press conference transcript", 24 April 2009, <http://helpsaveaware.blogspot.com/2009/04/23-april-2009-press-conference.html> [accessed 23 Nov. 2010].

"377A serves public morality: NMP Thio Li-Ann", 23 Oct. 2007, <http://theonlinecitizen.com/2007/10/377a-serves-public-morality-nmp-thio-li-ann> [accessed 23 Nov. 2010].

"An Extraordinary V Conference", 21 July 2009, <http://www.fifo.sg/post/show/329> [accessed 23 Nov. 2010].

Archer, Margaret, 2000, *Being human: the problem of agency*. Cambridge: Cambridge University Press.

"AWARE: gay agenda 'unfounded'", a press statement, 16 May 2009, <http://www.sgpolitics.net/?p=3029> [accessed 23 Nov. 2010].

"AWARE Old Guard's press conference, 24 Apr. 09", *Channel News Asia*, <http://www.youtube.com/watch?v=T6zyy11ppV0> [accessed 23 Nov. 2010].

"AWARE Roundtable Discussions", 27 Aug. 2010, <http://www.aware.org.sg/2010/08/round-table/> [accessed 23 Nov. 2010].

Cheong, Ace Kindred, "ST Forum: Wrong to say old EXCO promoted homo-sexuality", 25 April 2009, <http://www.we-are-aware.sg/2s009/04/25/ace-kindredcheong> [accessed 23 Nov. 2010].

DeLaet, Debra, "Gender and human rights discourse in the International Relations classroom: who speaks for whom", Paper prepared for presentation at the Annual Meeting of the International Studies Association in San Francisco, 25–30 March 2008, <http://www.allacademic.com//meta/p_mla_apa_research_citation/2/5/3/0/0/pages253005/p253005-1.php> [accessed 23 Nov. 2010].

Devasahayam, Theresa, 2011, "Contesting Feminisms: The AWARE Saga", in *The AWARE Saga: Civil Society and Public Morality in Singapore*, ed. Terence Chong. Singapore: NUS Press.

"Excerpts from AWARE press conference", *AsiaOne News*, 26 April 2009, <http://www.asiaone.com/News/AsiaOne%2BNews/Singapore/Story/A1Story20090426-137518.html> [accessed 23 Nov. 2010].

Gellner, Ernest, 1964, *Thought and change*. London: Weidenfeld and Nicolson.

"Get your AWARE 2009 EGM T-shirts", 4 May 2009, <http://mathialee.wordpress.com/2009/05/04/get-your-aware-2009-egm-t-shirts> [accessed 23 Nov. 2010].

Gouldner, Alvin, 1970, *The coming crisis of Western Sociology*. New York: Basic Books.

Hawkesworth, Mary, "When the subaltern speaks: transnational feminism and anti-racism politics", Paper prepared for presentation at the Annual Meeting of the American Political Science Association, Philadelphia, 29 Aug. 2003, <http://www.allacademic.com//meta/p_mla_apa_research_citation/0/6/3/6/7/pages63675/p63675-1.php> [accessed 23 Nov. 2010]

Lai Ah Eng, 2011, "Shut Up and Sit Down! Stand Up and Speak Out! The AWARE EGM as Performance of Civil Society in Singapore", in *The AWARE Saga: Civil Society and Public Morality in Singapore*, ed. Terence Chong. Singapore: NUS Press.

Lam, Dana, "ST letter by Dana Lam: AWARE has never had a 'gay agenda'", 16 May 2009, <http://www.sgpolitics.net/?p=3029> [accessed 23 Nov. 2010].

Law, Stephen, "Humanism and secularism", 1 Jan. 2010, <http://stephenlaw.blogspot.com/search?q=freedoms> [accessed 23 Nov. 2010].

Lemert, Charles and Paul Piccone, 1982, "Gouldner's theoretical method and reflexive sociology", *Theory and Society* 11, 6: 733–57.

"Letter to Dr John Chew", 15 May 2009, <http://www.we-are-aware.sg/2009/05/15/letter-to-dr-john-chew> [accessed 23 Nov. 2010].

Levesque-Lopman, Louise, 1989, "Seeing our seeing: Gouldner's reflexive socio-logy from a feminist phenomenological perspective", *The American Socio-logist* 20, 4: 362–72.

Lyons, Lenore, 2004, *A state of ambivalence: the Feminist Movement in Singapore*. Leiden: Brill.

Pearsall, Ronald, no date, *The worm in the bud: the world of Victorian sexuality*. London: Weidenfeld & Nicolson.

"Prime Minister Lee Hsien Loong's National Day Rally Speech 2009 on 16 August (Transcript)", <http://www.pmo.gov.sg/News/Messages/National+Day+Rally+Speech+2009+Part+3+Racial+and+Religious+Harmony.htm> [accessed 23 Nov. 2010].

rainbow harvest: proclaiming God's inclusive love, <http://www.psa91.com> [accessed 23 Nov. 2010].

"Sally Ang's 'shut up and sit down' incident at EGM", 2 May 2009, <http://www.youtube.com/watch?v=D-VYBZgwGdg> [accessed on 23 Nov. 2010].

"Save AWARE! Gender equality for all!", 22 April 2009, <http://www.gopetition.com/petitions/gender-equality-for-all.html> [accessed 23 Nov. 2010].

"SCWO acknowledgment of AWARE contribution", no date, <http://www.facebook.com/topic.php?uid=72296674515&topic=8006> [accessed 23 Nov. 2010].

"Shut up and sit down – the AWARE saga remixed", no date, <http://singapese.wordpress.com/2009/05/13/shut-up-and-sit-down-a-song-about-the-aware-egm> [accessed 23 Nov. 2010].

Soh Chin Ong, "Open letter: lessons for our secular nation", 4 May 2009, <http://www.we-are-aware.sg/2009/05/04/may-4-be-aware-lessons-for-our-secular-nation-by-ong-soh-chin> [accessed 23 Nov. 2010].

Singapore Penal Code, Chapter XVI (Offences Affecting the Human Body), Section 377 (Cap. 224), <http://statutes.agc.gov.sg/non_version/html/homepage.html> [accessed 23 Nov. 2010].

Seeh, Jarel, "ST Forum: Respect minorities", *The Straits Times*, 25 April 2009, <http://www.we-are-aware.sg/2009/04/25/april-25-published-st-forum-letter-by-jarel-seeh-respect-rights-of-minorities> [accessed 23 Nov. 2010].

Singam, Constance, "State's decisions a threat to secular society", 20 May 2010, <http://www.aware.org.sg/2010/05/states-decisions-a-threat-to-secular-society> [accessed 23 Nov. 2010].

"Statements of support from civil society groups", 30 April 2009, <http://www.we-are-aware.sg/2009/04/30/statements-of-support-from-civil-society-groups> [accessed 23 Nov. 2010].

"The AWARE saga", 2 May 2009, <http://www.we-are-aware.sg/2009/05/02/aware-saga> [accessed 23 Nov. 2010].

The Straits Times, 18 April 2009a, "Some attend the same church", by Tan Dawn Wei.

———, 18 April 2009b, "Who's who at the new AWARE and the questions they will not answer", text by Yen Feng and photos by Mugilan Rajasegeran.

"TOC exclusive: Constance Singam's letter to AWARE, in full", 19 April 2009, <http://theonlinecitizen.com/2009/04/toc-exclusive-constance-singam%E2%80%99s-letter-to-aware-in-full> [accessed 23 Nov. 2010].

"TOC breaking news: Old AWARE exco holds press conference, calls new AWARE 'moral vigilantes'", 24 April 2009, <http://theonlinecitizen. com/2009/04/toc-breaking-news-old-aware-exco-holds-press-conference-calls-new-aware-moral-vigilantes> [accessed 23 Nov. 2010].

"*Today*'s interview with DPM Wong Kan Seng on the AWARE saga", 15 May 2009, <http://www.sgpolitics.net/?p=3009> [accessed 23 Nov. 2010].

Truth, Sojourner, "Ain't I a woman?", Speech delivered at the Women's Convention in Akron, Ohio, 1851, <http://www.feminist.com/resources/artspeech/ genwom/sojour.htm> [accessed 23 Nov. 2010].

"'We cannot have people acting like moral vigilantes' says AWARE's old guards", 24 April 2009, <http://theonlinecitizen.com/2009/04/we-cannot-have-people-acting-like-moral-vigilantes-says-awares-old-guards> [accessed 23 Nov. 2010].

"Why neutral stance on homosexuals", 27 April 2009, <http://www.ngejay.com/ ?p=2595> [accessed 23 Nov. 2010].

Wink, Walter, no date, "Homosexuality and the Bible", <http://www.soulforce. org/article/homosexuality-bible-walter-wink> [accessed 23 Nov. 2010].

Contributors

Azhar Ghani is a risk consultant providing regional political economy and security assessments for businesses. Prior to his foray into risk consultancy, he was a journalist for eight years, including more than two years heading *The Straits Times*' Indonesian bureau in Jakarta. In between, he was a Research Fellow with the Institute of Policy Studies for two years before returning to full-time risk consulting. He spent another year as an Adjunct Research Associate with the Institute pursuing his research interests in multicultural and public policy issues in Singapore. He has also practised as an engineer.

Terence Chong is a Sociologist and Senior Fellow at the Institute of Southeast Asian Studies. His research areas are Singapore society, the sociology of culture, globalization studies and cultural policies in Singapore. He has published in *Modern Asian Studies*, *Journal of Contemporary Asia*, *Asian Studies Review*, *Critical Asian Studies*, among others. He is author of *The Theatre and the State in Singapore: Orthodoxy and Resistance* (Routledge, 2011) and editor of *Management of Success: Singapore Revisited* (ISEAS, 2010).

Chua Beng Huat is Provost's Professor, Faculty of Arts and Social Science. He is concurrently Head, Department of Sociology, Convenor Cultural Studies Programmes and Research Leader, Cultural Studies in Asia Research Cluster, Asia Research Institute, National University of Singapore. He has done conceptual ground breaking on Singapore politics, public housing policies and in cultural economy of East Asian pop cultures. He is founding co-executive editor of the journal, *Inter-Asia Cultural Studies*.

Dominic Chua is a creative consultant focused on strategic and public communications. His interest in civic society and the empowerment of disenfranchised groups has seen him involved with a number of different non-profit organisations, including TWC2, the Singapore

Anti-Death Penalty Group, and People Like Us. An English Language and Literature major, he has previously served as an educator in both public and private sector educational settings over the past decade.

Theresa W. Devasahayam is Fellow and Gender Studies Programme Coordinator at the Institute of Southeast Asian Studies. Her research areas include women migrants and HIV/AIDS, labour mobility, women and food security, and gender and ageing. She is co-author of *Gender, Emotions and Labour Markets: Asian and Western Perspectives* (London: Routledge, in press [with Ann Brooks]). Among her recent edited publications is *Singapore Women's Charter: Roles, Responsibilities and Rights in Marriage* (Singapore: Institute of Southeast Asian Studies, 2011), *Gender Trends in Southeast Asia: Women Now, Women in the Future* (Singapore: Institute of Southeast Asian Studies, 2009), and *Working and Mothering in Asia: Images, Ideologies and Identities* (Singapore and Copenhagen: NUS Press and Nordic Institute of Asian Studies, 2007) (with Brenda S.A. Yeoh). She has also published journal articles, book chapters, reports for international organizations, and book reviews on various women's issues.

Gillian Koh is a Senior Research Fellow at the Institute of Policy Studies. She contributes to the work in the Institute of Policy Studies' Politics and Governance cluster. The on-going research interests of the cluster include the nature of state-society relations and the development of civil society in Singapore; electoral politics; and the political values of Singaporeans. One other area the desk explores is the nature of social resilience of Singaporeans in the face of internal and external security threats. She is the Publications Coordinator at the Institute and the convenor of IPS' occasional Young Singaporeans Conference.

James Koh has been working in the education sector for the past nine years, both as a teacher and an administrator in a number of different schools. His research interests include educational programming for high-ability students, and the impact of introducing critical theory to high school students. An English Language and Literature graduate, he currently works in the area of corporate communications.

Lai Ah Eng is Senior Research Fellow at the Asia Research Institute and instructor at the University Scholars Programme, National University of Singapore. She has worked in various research capacities at the

Consumers' Association of Penang, Housing Development Board (Singapore), the National Archives of Singapore, Institute of Southeast Asian Studies (Singapore) and Institute of Policy Studies, and lectured at the Departments of Sociology and Social Work, National University of Singapore. Her research areas include multiculturalism, migration, family and heritage on which she has several major publications.

Loh Chee Kong is the News Editor at *TODAY* newspaper. As a reporter then, he had closely followed the developments at AWARE, reporting and observing firsthand how the media covered the saga. He takes a special interest in the development of the media and civil society in Singapore and regularly writes opinion pieces on related topics.

Eugene K.B. Tan is Assistant Law Professor at the School of Law, Singapore Management University. An advocate and solicitor of the Supreme Court of Singapore, Eugene Tan is a graduate of the National University of Singapore, the London School of Economics and Political Science, and Stanford University where he was a Fulbright Fellow. His inter-disciplinary research interests include the mutual interaction of law and public policy, and the regulation of ethnic conflict.

Alex Tham is a PhD candidate in Sociology at Princeton University. He is interested in the social conditions of knowledge, particularly how risk and uncertainty motivate action. Alex has an MSc in Applied Finance from Singapore Management University and an MA in Social Sciences from the University of Chicago. He has worked as a strategist at Singapore's Ministry of Trade and Industry, as a senior research analyst at the Ministry of Defence and was a research associate at the Institute of Southeast Asian Studies.

Jack Yong has been a journalist for the past six years in broadcast and web publishing. A business management graduate, he is currently a writer/editor by day, a postgraduate student by night. His research interests include political communications and media effects.

Vivienne Wee is an anthropologist who has done extensive research on issues of gender, power, religion, and ethno-nationalism, especially in Indonesia. She taught at the National University of Singapore, The Chinese University of Hong Kong and City University of Hong Kong. She was Director of the Research Programme Consortium on Women's

Empowerment in Muslim Contexts in 2006–9, which was supported by the Department for International Development, UK. She is currently a research consultant with Women Reclaiming and Re-defining Culture, a programme coordinated by Women Living Under Muslim Laws and the Institute for Women's Empowerment, supported by the MDG3 Fund of the Netherlands Government. As a public intellectual, she has worked to enhance a more participatory and holistic understanding of development issues and processes, through collaboration with other academic researchers, civil society organisations, local communities, as well as international development agencies. She is a founder and life member of AWARE in Singapore.

Index